STUDENT UNIT GUIDE

AS English Language & Literature
UNIT 3

AQA
Specification B

Module 3: Production of Texts

Linda Varley

Series Editor: John Shuttleworth

Philip Allan Updates
Market Place
Deddington
Oxfordshire
OX15 0SE

Orders
Bookpoint Ltd, 130 Milton Park, Abingdon, Oxfordshire, OX14 4SB
tel: 01235 827720
fax: 01235 400454
e-mail: uk.orders@bookpoint.co.uk
Lines are open 9.00 a.m.–5.00 p.m., Monday to Saturday, with a 24-hour message answering service. You can also order through the Philip Allan Updates website:
www.philipallan.co.uk

© Philip Allan Updates 2006

ISBN-13: 978-1-84489-560-1
ISBN-10: 1-84489-560-2

All rights reserved; no part of this publication may be reproduced, stored in a retrieval system, or transmitted, in any form or by any means, electronic, mechanical, photocopying, recording or otherwise without either the prior written permission of Philip Allan Updates or a licence permitting restricted copying in the United Kingdom issued by the Copyright Licensing Agency Ltd, 90 Tottenham Court Road, London W1T 4LP.

This guide has been written specifically to support students preparing for AQA Specification B English Language and Literature Unit 3 coursework. The content has been neither approved nor endorsed by AQA and remains the sole responsibility of the author.

Printed by MPG Books, Bodmin

Contents

Introduction

About this guide 4

Studying English Language and Literature 4

Unit 3 specification 5

How your folder is marked 7

Assessment objectives 7

How to present your coursework folder 13

■ ■ ■

Content Guidance

About this section 16

Writing to entertain 17

Writing to persuade 26

Writing to inform 34

Writing to advise/instruct 43

Commentary writing 50

■ ■ ■

Student Coursework

About this section 56

A-grade reading text 57

C-grade reading text 63

A-grade listening text 68

C-grade listening text 74

Introduction

About this guide

The aim of this guide is to help you prepare the Unit 3 coursework of AQA Specification B English Language and Literature. It covers the main areas of the coursework folder and is intended to support the teaching that you will receive for this unit. There are three sections to this guide:

(1) **Introduction** — this outlines the Unit 3 specification and explains the key points that you need to understand to be able to complete your coursework folder.

(2) **Content Guidance** — this provides a guide to a range of ideas and skills that you may use to produce a successful coursework folder. It contains advice and includes activities that will prepare you for writing your own texts and commentaries.

(3) **Student Coursework** — this includes examples of A- and C-grade texts and their accompanying commentaries produced by students. These are interspersed with comments from the moderator, which highlight both the strengths and the areas for development in each text and commentary.

Studying English Language and Literature

Unit 3 is the coursework component of the AS course. It was designed to allow you to develop your own ideas and interests as you practise your writing skills. For this unit, you can choose the aspects you particularly enjoy and want to develop, because it is understood that not everyone has the same skills, interests or inclination to write in the same way.

A-level English Language and Literature builds on your GCSE coursework, for which you might have had to present an argument or write a short story. In the A-level course, you can experiment with a range of writing tasks before submitting your final texts.

This course differs from GCSE because you are required to write a commentary to accompany each text, explaining the purpose and process of your writing. This requires you to analyse your own language and to be aware of how language is used in any style models that might have influenced your approach to writing your own text.

Sometimes students struggle with the idea of free choice when beginning their coursework, as you can see from the following comments, which reflect the two differing approaches of students to coursework:
- 'If you tell me what to write, I'll write it.'
- 'I don't have anything to write about.'

But more often students welcome the opportunity to develop their own writing:
- 'I've got lots of ideas for stories. I'm always writing them.'

- 'I already review computer games for the internet. Can I use that?' (The answer is 'Yes'.)

You can work on coursework in your own time, without the time pressure of an exam. You can redraft texts after feedback from your teacher (and others) and the coursework is submitted well before the examination revision timetable gets under way.

You need to remember that coursework takes up a lot of time. You have to be organised: time-management skills are crucial, especially if other subjects also involve coursework and the deadlines are close together. You must sustain your involvement in your writing; you will not achieve a good overall mark if you work hard on one text but do not spend much time on the second.

You must also understand that the total number of marks available is split evenly between texts (50%) and commentaries (50%). You will probably enjoy writing your texts and spend a considerable amount of time on them. However, in order to improve your whole folder you must spend an equal amount of time reflecting on and analysing your work for the accompanying commentary.

The English Language and Literature coursework helps you to develop your writing expertise and analytical skills. If you continue into A2, you will find it excellent preparation for the Unit 4 coursework (Text Transformation). In fact, most students say that they understand what is required for text transformation because they have completed the AS coursework. Even if you decide not to continue your English studies after AS, you will have developed some important skills. You may take up a career in journalism — or even write a novel.

Using your knowledge and experience is one of the best ways of starting to think about what to write. Many of the examples contained in this guide started out as the knowledge, interest or experience of the student concerned.

Useful questions to consider when thinking about what to write include:
- What do you do in your leisure time?
- Do you belong to any clubs or groups?
- Do you have any hobbies or skills?
- Do you have a part-time job?
- Are you interested in reading, music or films?

The answer to one of the above questions may be the start of an idea that you could use for one of the texts in your coursework folder.

Unit 3 specification

You will find it useful to have a straightforward guide to the requirements for this module. There are five key areas of assessment:

(1) One text must be written primarily for a reading audience and another primarily for a listening audience.

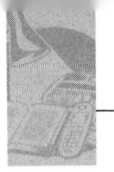

You may find that you are more familiar with writing for a reading audience (a short story, leaflet, booklet, magazine article etc.) than you are with scripting for a listening audience (monologue, radio drama, television script, audio guide, speech, talk etc.) The Content Guidance section looks at writing for both a reading and a listening audience, with advice and tips. When writing for a listening audience it is important to remember that you must produce a written text for someone to perform — it should not be a transcription of natural speech. Therefore, you cannot write a phone-in, an interview, a commentary (e.g. of a football match or news report) or anything else that is taking place at the same time that the report is being made.

(2) The total length of the two texts should be between 1,500 and 3,000 words.

The word count is part of the rubric (rules), just as taking an examination in a stipulated time is, so you must comply with these regulations. The range in the permitted number of words is intended to allow you to explore writing that may require more length (such as a short story, a play script or a monologue) or that needs to be shorter because the effectiveness would be reduced if it were too long (such as an opinion piece in the media or an advertising campaign).

(3) The total length of the commentary (or commentaries) should be between 1,000 and 1,500 words.

Your two texts should be accompanied by a commentary that analyses and reviews what you have produced. Most students submit two commentaries, dealing separately with each text, rather than one combined commentary. The commentary involves reflection on such matters as genre, sentence structure, rhetorical effects and structure of text (see pp. 50–54 in the Content Guidance section). Writing the commentary will support your analytical work for Unit 1 as well as forming a basis for the A2 units.

(4) Each text should be differentiated in terms of primary purpose, audience and genre.

- **Primary purpose** — the specification indicates four primary purposes: to entertain, to persuade, to inform and to advise/instruct. These purposes are dealt with on pp. 17–49 of the Content Guidance section. You are required to identify a primary purpose in the commentary, although secondary purposes may also be indicated. For example, if you write to persuade, you may include information, since selected facts will support the persuasion.
- **Audience** — you must differentiate the audiences of your two texts. The most successful students identify audiences by interest or target group rather than in generalised terms of 'adults' or 'everyone' (or even 'those middle-aged people over 35'). When writing for children, you need to be aware of the differing demands of the range of Key Stages (see pp. 35–39 for information about writing for Key Stage 1 and Key Stage 2). The best possible preparation for such writing is arranging a visit to a school, reading the books that children read and testing your text on the target audience.
- **Genre** — it is unlikely that you will duplicate the same genre for each text. For example, a magazine article could not be presented to a listening audience.

You may wish to submit a monologue for your listening text and a first-person short story for the reading text. However, these are linked too closely to be acceptable, and they are both likely to be written to entertain, which is also unacceptable.

(5) The adoption of any genre.

The specification advises you to choose writing tasks that reflect your interests. You are less likely to be engaged in writing for a 'set task' and as a result you may achieve a higher mark by following your interests.

The table below summarises the requirements for the Unit 3 coursework.

Text 1 — for a reading audience	Commentary for Text 1
Purpose: one of entertain; persuade; inform; instruct/advise	
Audience: any	
Text 2 — for a listening audience	Commentary for Text 2
Purpose: a different one of entertain; persuade; inform; instruct/advise	
Audience: any except the one used for Text 1	
Total word count for the two texts = 1,500–3,000 words	Total word count for the two commentaries = 1,000–1,500 words

How your folder is marked

Your folder will be marked first by your teacher, who will award a mark out of 30 for the two texts, balancing the strengths and weaknesses of each piece of work. The same process (with a mark out of 30) is used for marking the commentary/commentaries. The total mark for your folder is therefore out of 60.

It is likely that your folder will be marked again by at least one other teacher from your school, and they will discuss and standardise the folders before sending the marks (and folders) to a moderator. The moderator is a neutral person employed by the examination board to ensure that every centre marks to the same standard — which makes the whole process of coursework part of the examination 'system'. Usually, moderators will confirm the marks you have been given, although they have the power to raise or lower the marks in order to standardise the process.

Assessment objectives

Assessment objectives are the particular areas of knowledge, understanding and skills that you have to meet.

Texts

The assessment objectives that apply to Unit 3 texts are listed in the table on p. 8.

AO4	Show understanding of the ways contextual variation and choices of form, style and vocabulary shape the meanings of texts.
AO6	Demonstrate expertise and accuracy in writing for a variety of specific purposes and audiences, drawing on the knowledge of literary texts and linguistic features to explain and comment on the choices made.

It may be useful to consider what these assessment objectives actually mean:

AO4	You have to write in your chosen genres so that vocabulary and content are perfectly matched to audience, purpose and mode.
AO6	You must show that you can write with control and accuracy; choose different audiences and purposes; and understand the difference between writing for a reading and a listening audience.

As a result, marks are awarded for texts that show originality, have control of form and style, are matched to audience and purpose and show control in crafting texts for both a reading audience and a listening audience. This may sound impossible, but if you look at the Student Coursework section, you will realise that these criteria are achievable.

Assessment criteria

The table below lists the criteria that must be met for AO4 and AO6 in each mark band.

0–5 marks	
AO4	Some evidence of considered choices of form and meanings.
AO6	Some rudimentary knowledge of genre requirements, some identifiable features of writing for different purposes and audiences.
6–10 marks	
AO4	Some awareness of variation in some aspect of form and style which have an effect on meaning.
AO6	Some awareness of genre requirements and of variables when writing for different audiences and purposes.
11–15 marks	
AO4	Awareness and some understanding of variation in some aspects of form and style which have an effect on meaning.
AO6	Some control of genre requirements and of variables when writing for different audiences and purposes.
16–20 marks	
AO4	Shows an informed understanding of form and style which have an effect on meaning.
AO6	Control of genre requirements and of variables when writing for different audiences and purposes.
21–25 marks	
AO4	Shows a detailed and informed understanding of form and style which have an effect on meaning.

AQA (B) Unit 3

AO6	Firm control of genre requirements and of variables when writing for different audiences and purposes.
26–30 marks AO4 AO6	Consistent and sophisticated control of form and style to create some subtle meanings. Very assured control of genre and of variables when writing for different audiences and purposes.

These criteria are written in a formal language that sometimes requires decoding. The following explanation is more straightforward. The comment opposite the marks gives an overview of each mark band.

0–5 marks	**Inadequate fulfilment** • a very weak submission • incomplete • intrusive weaknesses in technical presentation • loss of control of language and form • no sense of audience, purpose and mode
6–10 marks	**Basic fulfilment** • infringements of key areas of assessment • beginnings of variety in vocabulary and syntax • no identifiable voice • beginning to lose control of language and form • some sense of purpose, audience and mode
11–15 marks	**Some competence** • loose control of genre or heavy reliance on style model • more conscious use of vocabulary and syntax • predictable choices and treatment of material • technical control not complete • attempts to suit needs of audience, purpose and mode
16–20 marks	**Competent work** • an even balance of strengths and weaknesses • less adventurous and more formulaic writing • increasing sophistication in vocabulary and syntax • writes in different genres but often addresses a narrower range of audiences • occasional technical lapses that do not inhibit required response • clear identification of purpose, audience and mode
21–25 marks	**Good work** • interesting and/or well researched • achieves a good level of success • form, content and style consistently matched to audience, purpose and mode • fluent, coherently structured writing that shows evidence of conscious crafting • may include one text of the highest standard and a second text that is more predictable, formulaic and less demanding

AS English Language & Literature

26–30 marks	**Excellent work**
	• clearly original and imaginative
	• challenging, adventurous and successful writing
	• fulfils criterion of sophisticated control
	• form, content and style assuredly matched to audience, purpose and mode
	• high level of technical accuracy
	• consistent and distinctive style that shows evidence of controlled and sustained crafting

Each mark band is approximately equivalent to an AS grade, with 26–30 a grade A and 0–5 a fail.

Commentaries

The assessment objectives that apply to Unit 3 commentaries are listed in the table below.

AO4	Show understanding of the ways contextual variation and choices of form, style and vocabulary shape the meanings of texts.
AO5	Identify and consider the ways attitudes and values are created in speech and writing.
AO6	Demonstrate expertise and accuracy in writing for a variety of specific purposes and audiences, drawing on the knowledge of literary texts and linguistic features to explain and comment on the choices made.

As with the texts, it is helpful to consider what these assessment objectives actually mean:

AO4	Your commentary should show an understanding of the vocabulary and sentence structures that you used.
AO5	You need to refer to sources and style models (if used) and indicate how they influenced the way you wrote. You also need to discuss decisions that you made in the course of your writing, particularly for crafting a text for a reading audience and scripting a text for a listening audience.
AO6	Your focus here is purpose and audience, and you should show what changes you made in drafting as a result of this focus.

You are awarded marks for the commentary:
- when you can show an accurate and appropriate analysis of your own language use
- when drafting has been undertaken to good effect
- when sources and style models are used and referred to, and appropriate audience testing has not only been undertaken but it has informed any changes that you might have made

Assessment objective 5 (AO5) requires you to show a clear understanding of the differences between writing for a reading audience and a listening audience.

Students are often concerned about writing their commentary — advice is given on how to deal with commentary writing on pp. 50–54 of the Content Guidance section. Examples of students' commentaries are given in the Student Coursework section. You must remember that the assessment objectives can be achieved if you follow the advice of your teachers and allow time for discussion of your commentary with them. The best commentaries are planned in good time and are not left until the last minute.

Assessment criteria

The table below lists the criteria that must be met for AO4, AO5 and AO6 in each mark band.

0–5 marks	
AO4	Rudimentary awareness of choices of form and style.
AO5	Attempts to comment on attitudes and values.
AO6	Some attempt to consider purpose, audience and own use of language.

6–10 marks	
AO4	Some awareness of choices of form and style and how they shape meaning.
AO5	Some awareness of how attitudes and values are created and conveyed.
AO6	Comments on own language use.

11–15 marks	
AO4	Some comment on own choices of form and style and how they shape meanings.
AO5	Identification of attitudes and values in the two pieces and consideration of how these are created and conveyed.
AO6	Comments on own language use by drawing on linguistic knowledge.

16–20 marks	
AO4	Description of own choices of form and style and how they shape meanings.
AO5	Understanding of some methods used to create and convey specific attitudes and values.
AO6	Some developed comment on own language use, based on linguistic knowledge.

21–25 marks	
AO4	Understanding and explanation of choices of form and style and how they shape meaning.
AO5	Some description and explanation of specific methods used to create and convey attitudes and values.
AO6	Detailed comments on own language use, drawing on linguistic knowledge.

26–30 marks	
AO4	Assured understanding and explanation of choices of form and style and how they shape meaning.
AO5	Sustained and assured discussion of specific choices made to create and convey attitudes and values.
AO6	Comments effectively and in detail on a range of features of own choices and language use.

These criteria are written in a formal language that sometimes requires decoding. The following explanation is more straightforward. The comment opposite the marks gives an overview of each mark band.

0–5 marks	**Inadequate fulfilment** • very brief • perfunctory description and summary of tasks • simple statements • no progression from GCSE standard
6–10 marks	**Basic fulfilment** • brief • fails to explain the process of writing • anecdotal or continues to discuss the content of the text • comments on own language use without understanding terminology • little evidence of redrafting • emphasis on surface features such as graphology rather than on language
11–15 marks	**Some competence** • descriptive • anecdotal • if present, linguistic features simply catalogued or inappropriately identified • may be dependent on source material without showing an awareness • concentration on graphology rather than language features
16–20 marks	**Competent work** • a balance between descriptive and analytical writing • tendency to list rather than explore linguistic features • cursory reference to the process of drafting • tendency to brevity
21–25 marks	**Good work** • appropriate use of terminology • addresses audience and purpose clearly • refers to the redrafting process • acknowledges sources and style models • self-aware and critical • more analytical than descriptive • exemplifies from own writing • some awareness of objectivity in authorial voice • addresses the issue of writing for a reading and listening audience
26–30 marks	**Excellent work** • appropriate and accurate use of terminology • refers to redrafting and discusses the effects of decisions made in the redrafting process on changes made in the text • acknowledges sources and style models (where appropriate) and explains how they have influenced decisions in writing • appropriate and impartial audience testing • shows awareness of success in achieving stated purpose • objectivity in authorial voice • analyses own language use in detail • refers appropriately to the demands of differentiation of writing for a reading and a listening audience

AQA (B) Unit 3

How to present your coursework folder

Your folder should be presented so that the texts and commentary/commentaries are easily accessible and all your work is kept together. Thin plastic files, document wallets, large envelopes and plastic wallets are recommended. Do not place all of your work in a single plastic wallet or in a hard PVC ring binder.

The best way to present your work is in the following order:
- Candidate Record Form — make sure you have signed it to confirm that it is your own work.
- Final draft of reading text — it helps if this is labelled clearly as your final draft.
- The accompanying commentary to your reading text.
- Bibliography, source material and style model for the reading text — label them and insert them immediately after your reading text and commentary.
- Rough drafts of reading text, starting with the first draft (indicate clearly as 'first draft, second draft etc.'). Moderators will look at your first draft to assess how much your text has progressed.
- Final draft of listening text — again labelled clearly.
- The accompanying commentary to your listening text.
- Bibliography, source material and style model for the listening text — again labelled clearly.
- Rough drafts of listening text, again starting with the first draft.
- If you are including any audio cassettes, disks or videos they should be of standard size.
- If you have researched on the internet, you should submit hard copies of the website pages — you will have had to print them when planning your drafts and they will allow you to show how you crafted the text.

Content Guidance

This section deals with the four purposes indicated in the specification: writing to entertain, persuade, inform and instruct/advise. For each purpose, advice is given on writing for a reading audience and scripting for a listening audience. The section concludes with guidance on writing a commentary.

It is difficult to consider the four purposes without talking about a specific task and audience, so the following have been used for clarification:

(1) entertain — writing detective genre stories, plays and dramas
(2) persuade — writing about animal/environmental charities
(3) inform — teaching primary school children about the Great Fire of London
(4) instruct/advise — offering advice for AS students

Examples of successful writing are listed at the beginning of each purpose. You should look at these suggestions, because they may trigger an idea for you. If not, you will need to think of other ways to collect ideas.

It is important to remember that the examples given in this section are not the only types of writing that you can submit. The best writing will always be what you choose to write and what interests you.

Writing to entertain

Writing for a reading audience

The following ideas have been used successfully by previous students. Look at the list below and consider whether there are any ideas that you might be happy to try:
- short stories based on a genre you admire, e.g. detective, fantasy, thriller, sci-fi
- a General Studies guide to Greek myths
- a photostory with a convincing narrative
- journalism and feature writing

Many students have the impression that writing to entertain requires them to write a short story. As you can see from the list above, writing a short story is only one of a number of options, but it is a popular choice. Although it is not the only, or the best, choice of writing to entertain, the short-story form is used in this section as an example to explain how you could plan your own writing.

Crafting your own story is an ideal opportunity to show your knowledge of style models, since you will be writing in a genre that you know and, presumably, read a lot. Your study of the paired texts for Unit 2 will have informed you of a specific genre and you may choose this as your style model. For example, if you studied *The Hound of the Baskervilles* by Sir Arthur Conan Doyle, and *The No.1 Ladies' Detective Agency* by Alexander McCall Smith, you will be familiar with the detective genre. You may therefore choose this genre as a style model for writing a short detective story.

Writing a short detective story

The detective genre, narrated by a companion of a private, amateur detective who is more observant than the local police force, was invented by the American author Edgar Allan Poe. The detective was able to solve mysteries in which people were killed in locked rooms or where he discovered hidden, but important, letters through logical deduction. Sir Arthur Conan Doyle developed the investigative expertise of the fictional detective, creating an eccentric but logical and analytical Sherlock Holmes. Many authors took up the genre, and the popularity of the fictional detective continues to the present day. Writing in 2001, Alexander McCall Smith used his personal knowledge of Africa to set the location of his stories about Mma Ramotswe, a Botswana patriot who uses her African common sense to solve people's problems.

The following sections look at the four key areas of writing a short story.

Beginnings
It is essential to create atmosphere and setting, as well as establishing character, from the very beginning of a short story. The short-story form is too brief to allow a more leisurely approach.

Read the following extract written by Sally Jones, a student:

> I will never forget her face. It was so serene, peaceful and still. The water lapping gently over her bluing features. My sister. My sister was always the centre of my life, and I of hers. I was the only one she could talk to. I drew her lifeless body out of the water with gentle care. It was effortless; she was so light and fragile. In utter horror I saw that her body was severed below the navel, there was just nothing there. I ran. Back to the house. In a haze, stumbling over every twig on the way, unconscious of the fact that I was leaving a stream of vomit the entire distance. I haven't ventured near the lake since then and can't imagine ever doing so. The next day another half body was recovered from the lake, lying between the reeds in the marshy sludge, the police had found it in the opposite end of the lake to where my sister was found. The lower half of a male. Also severed at the navel.
>
> The trauma counsellor has suggested that I write down my thoughts to vent my emotions, so here I will document the investigation so far: it has only been a week since I found her body.
>
> ### Sally's commentary
> My intention is to engage the reader and encourage him/her to read on. I decided to start with the finding of the bodies to both shock and intrigue the reader. Making the bodies severed in half is quite shocking and horrific, so the reader may think that for such a horrific murder there must be an interesting reason behind it, especially as there were two bodies, one male, one female. I thought that this beginning would provoke a lot of questions in the reader, such as why was the narrator's sister killed? Why in such a horrific manner? Whose is the second body and is he connected to the first body? It is intended therefore that suspense is created and the reader will want to find out the answer to these questions. In order to reflect the shocking circumstances and the emotion of the narrator I made the sentences quite short.
>
> I made the narrative that of someone directly involved with the victim of the crime, the brother, so that once the narrator has brought the reader up to date with the recent happenings they will discover the rest of the findings of the investigation at the same time as the narrator.

Setting/place

All stories have some kind of setting. Setting is a vital component of the narrative since it evokes the atmosphere in which the characters exist and in which the story occurs. In doing so, setting is an integral part of both.

An indication of the importance of setting is that for some writers, the creation of the story begins with an idea of place. Conan Doyle usually located his stories in London, although *The Hound of the Baskervilles* has a Gothic setting on isolated moorland. McCall Smith uses his own experience of Africa to place Mma Ramotswe in Botswana, and the setting plays an important part in his stories.

Read the following passage, again written by Sally:

In the summer the lake and the woods surrounding it were a place of laughter and fun. The perfect location for hide and seek. My sister and I were never bored in the summer holidays. It was an idyllic place to be brought up and it was from the long hours spent in the grounds of our house that our love of nature arose. Now the thought of going down there fills me with dread. The day I found my sister's body was cool and overcast and it had started to rain. I was taking a walk to clear my head after an argument with my father who had been in a particularly bad mood. Our relationship, never warm, was slowly but surely deteriorating, mostly due to his constant criticism of my much loved sister. The woods in winter are quite eerie; a kind of wispy, menacing fog seems to settle around the base of the trees as it spills off the lake. The boughs of the trees seem heavy and stoop threateningly, the mist distorting their shapes to create unnatural images. From a distance I thought the body in the lake was a fallen bough. In an instant, it seemed, I was surrounded by darkness. The trees seemed to bow lower and enclose me. The wind grew louder and roared through the leafless branches. Even the lake created an unbearable rushing sound through my ears.

Sally's commentary

The setting describes the place where the narrator finds his sister's body. I chose the setting of a lake surrounded by a wood as I thought it lends itself to the creation of an appropriate atmosphere of suspense and isolation. The fact that the body was found in the lake in the grounds of the girl's actual home contributes to the atmosphere of mystery.

I included a contrast of how the area seemed during happy summer times to reflect how the setting appeared on the day the body was found and to emphasise the sinister situation.

Presenting the characters

In short stories the characters must be presented to the reader immediately. The 'thumbnail sketch' is a valuable technique and its brevity encourages active readership.

Characters can be presented and described in a variety of ways:
- statement
- suggestion
- appearance
- action
- comparisons
- speech

A writer may use any combination of these.

Read the following description of the detective from Sally's story:

I had known Anthony McGuire since our days at university. He was very popular and renowned as the joker of our halls. As he emerged from the car and in spite of the seriousness of the situation I couldn't help but observe that he still had a revolting taste in ties. On further observation, however, I noted the deeply etched lines in his grave face and the prematurely greying hair. This appearance did not match the fun-loving character I knew him to have years before. It was painfully obvious that his years of having to deal with dead bodies and desperate families had subdued his appetite for fun and scarred his emotions. He obviously recognised me and for a split second I saw the glimmer of a smile on his stern face as he inevitably remembered some light-hearted incident from our past. His features returned to their serious expression as he realised the circumstances under which he regained my acquaintance and his eyes became sorrowful as he greeted me. He had fleetingly met my sister, I remember, when she came to visit me one autumn at university. I don't know if he remembered her or not, we didn't reminisce. I don't think I will ever be able to think of memories fondly without a big black cloud of guilt hanging over me for daring to be happy for a moment. Everything seems so inconsequential now.

McGuire was extremely thorough, every little detail seemed important to him. He wanted to know everything about her character and life, her relationships, even her favourite food. Every little detail. His questioning took up so much time; I couldn't help but wish he would stop asking trivial questions and give me some answers. To every question he seemed to assign so much importance to the reply. His serious enthusiasm for the importance of each answer made me think he was about to reveal the entire mystery. His confidence and enthusiasm gave me the belief that he would solve the crime and allow life to somehow continue.

Sally's commentary

I have chosen to describe the character of the detective because this character is more involved with the formation of the story; the villain plays only a small part in the story because the narration takes place after the crime has already been committed. The detective takes an active, crucial role in the unravelling of the investigation and plot.

By making the detective a former friend of the narrator the description of the detective can be much more insightful. There is a background and the narrator can give comments on his contrast in character and behaviour and can more reliably theorise on the emotional and character change that detective work has promoted in him. If I had chosen a detective who was unknown to the narrator, it would have meant that the friend was unqualified to give a reliable opinion of his personality. The description therefore would have been mainly with the detective's physical description or behaviour in an isolated incident. I have chosen instead to have a character who would add depth to the story.

Structure and plot

It is important to consider how to structure the plot of your story. This is vital planning, which you should refer to in your commentary.

The plot consists of the plan, design, scheme or pattern of events. It is the organisation of incident or character in such a way as to induce curiosity and suspense in the reader.

There are four elements of a traditional short story:
- **exposition** — the part of the story that sets the scene and introduces characters
- **complication** — the part of the story in which the lives of the characters are complicated in some way
- **climax** — the point at which the suspense is highest and matters are most threatening
- **resolution** — a solution for the complication is introduced; it may not be a happy one

Waiting for inspiration?

The hardest part of writing a short story can be coming up with a plot. Local or national newspapers often carry small stories that are, in effect, the outline of a plot. Collect some examples and consider whether there is a story that could be fleshed out as a result. Below are two examples:

Third surfer found dead on Cornish beach

A surfer who gave up university to pursue his hobby as a career has died on a beach in Cornwall. C__F__, 21, is the third surfer to lose his life on Cornwall's beaches in the past 3 weeks.

Mr F__, who lived in Newquay, went surfing on Wednesday afternoon off Towan Beach, Newquay. His body was discovered on another beach the next day.

Murder mystery in *Midsomer* village

A murder mystery is under way in a village used as a setting for the *Midsomer Murders* television series, after a man was found killed by a bullet to his neck.

When the body of G__M__ was discovered on Monday, slumped at the wheel of his car, there was no immediate evidence to suggest foul play.

Writing for a listening audience

The list below shows some successful pieces of work that have been submitted by students writing to entertain for a listening audience. Look at the list and consider whether there are any ideas that you may like to try:
- a Radio 4 drama
- a monologue for radio with appropriate scripting
- a television script
- play and pantomime scripts

The following sections focus on developing writing skills and the different methods required to produce scripts for plays and for radio dramas.

Play writing

What do you think is distinctive about writing plays as opposed to other forms of writing? Consider the following points:
- Unlike in a short story, the written word in a play is not the final product. When we talk of a play, we mean the performance as much as the script. And there are many intermediaries between you (the writer) and the director, designer and actors. You may not be present to offer advice or control their interpretation, so the performance may change your original beyond recognition.
- The importance of strong dialogue or talk. Talk may be incidental in a short story or novel, but plays rely almost entirely on talk to tell the story, propel the plot forward and develop characters.

The following sections look at the key elements of writing a play.

Talk

Some writers find it easier to script talk than narrative — having a speaker in mind helps to focus their writing. However, you need a high degree of 'word power' to use talk as a way of developing and providing all the necessary background information.

Once you have scripted the talk, read it aloud — this is the best test of 'performability'. It helps if you can find someone who is happy to read the script with you so that you can assess if the talk works and if it conveys the characters you had imagined.

Tone

As a playwright, you need to be alert to the way in which people speak to each other in a variety of environments — for example, on a bus, at a club, within a family.

One useful technique for developing sensitivity to tone is to write a dialogue between people of different age groups, adjusting the content and the manner of speech accordingly. Avoid the temptation to write as *you* would speak, rather than as your characters would speak.

How to start

Think about the construction of a play on a modest scale. To keep it compact, use a single unit with no time lapses or scene changes, containing it within a single act.

Choose a plot or a story line
You could choose to:
- base your play on fact
- write a mystery play — perhaps a whodunnit
- present a slice of real life — this is more difficult than it sounds, since a play needs definite structure and real life tends to be more chaotic

Do not make your plot or story line too complicated.

Conflict
Every piece of theatre needs conflict. There must be something that promotes action: a problem to resolve, an obstacle to overcome or a threat to be evaded.

You may find it unproductive simply to sit down and try to construct a plot. If so, think about a plot over a period of a few days. Make a note of ideas and situations that you feel have dramatic potential.

Starting to write
Once you have decided on an outline plot, you can start to write. Remember to pace your writing; you need to build up your story gradually. You should not disclose the whole story minutes after curtain up, or save all the action until the last few minutes. As a simple guide for a successful first attempt you could:
- catch your audience's attention with your opening
- proceed through perhaps two or three major climaxes
- reach a final climax that will resolve the whole play and leave the audience with a sense of resolution

Preparing the character list
The characters will have suggested themselves as you build up the plot, but you need to include as part of your submission a character list along with a description of where and when the action takes place.

General advice to novice writers is to avoid attempting to write too detailed a description. The particular attributes of your characters can be left to emerge from the talk and the plot.

Setting the scene
The next task is to decide where and when the action of your play takes place. If you are writing a one-act play without scene changes, then obviously this is an immediate limitation. However, remember that although the scene is static, the characters are not: they can enter and leave. They can also describe off-stage events through their dialogue — Shakespeare sometimes used this device to avoid the need to stage battle scenes.

As the play will be of short duration and the scene will be constant, you should control your 'time' element. For example, if you want the audience to learn of past events, you should rely on characters to deliver this information by discussing events that happened last week or last year.

Stage directions: help or hindrance?
A stage direction is a description of the movement or positioning of your actors, or of sound, scenic or lighting effects. Your stage directions can ensure how the scene is set, giving precise descriptions and a comprehensive set of instructions for the actors.

However, there is a danger when writing stage directions. If you specify where and when the action takes place, you may find that you have provided details that should emerge instead from the dialogue. Information that should be in the script can all too easily appear alongside it, for the eyes of the director rather than the enjoyment of the audience.

Hints

Remember the following points when attempting to bring characters to life:
- Do not waste words on lengthy introductions. Set the scene briefly and move straight into the action — let the scene unfold as you write.
- Give your main characters an early appearance. Remember that it is possible to give the audience information about a character before he/she appears on stage, by using the words of other characters.
- Let the story develop through your characters. Let them enter gradually; this will enable the story line to be passed from one to another — rather like a relay race with the story line as the baton.

The focus of this section has been on writing a play script for the stage. This is a logical point to start from when scripting for a listening audience, since a play can be acted out to evaluate its effectiveness.

A development of this scripting is to write for radio, which is an extension of scripting for the theatre.

Writing radio drama

Radio is a distinctive means of communication with its own limitations and possibilities and its own particular techniques. Anyone who wishes to write for radio must be familiar with its existing output.

The best way to become familiar with the possibilities of the medium is to listen to radio plays as often as possible, and decide what works and what does not. You will notice how radio drama works to keep the listener attentive, capturing the mood in the first minute. This does not mean that there is not time for the slow build, but the radio play should still have something that people can get interested in from the start.

Hints
- The only way to establish a character's presence is for him/her to speak or be referred to by name. If you put too many characters in a scene, the listener will lose track.
- Avoid putting in stage directions for the benefit of the producer or the actors. If it is important, it should be there in the dialogue.
- Sound effects should work with the dialogue. They are useful in setting a scene, but they must be subtle. A variety of sound is essential for holding the listener's attention and engaging his/her imagination.
- Character names should always be given in full and clearly separated from speech, as should sound effects and other technical information.
- Do not put several scenes in a row in the same location — listeners are interested by variety.
- Do not end Scene 1 with same speaker who begins Scene 2.
- Do not write all the scenes of the same length — juxtaposition of length is important to maintain audience interest.

AQA (B) Unit 3

Sound effects

Sound effects are used to add colour — they can show the listener what is happening, and without them you would need to use a narrator.

Look at the following example of a detective thriller written for radio by an AS student.

> FX birdsong
>
> FX sound of footsteps
>
> FX background traffic

ADAM STEEL: Herald Tribune, please.

NEWSVENDOR: There you go.

ADAM STEEL: Thank you.

> FX rustle of paper

ADAM STEEL: Oh God.

ADAM STEEL: *(reading aloud in an undertone)* Captain Adam Steel, who recently resigned his commission from the Royal Wessex Regiment, is being sought by police following the murder of…

> FX police car siren in distance

ADAM STEEL: No time to be on the streets.

> FX sound of church bells

ADAM STEEL: Ahh. The cathedral.

> FX fade of police car siren and traffic noise
>
> FX change of acoustics; echo effect of footsteps

ADAM STEEL: *(quietly)* Act naturally. Kneel and pray.

This extract is a good example of how sound effects can be used to convince your listening audience of the believability of your radio play.

The action taking place in the play has been facilitated by the sound effects. The audience hears, but is not told, that Adam Steel has sought refuge off the streets and avoided possible discovery by the police. For example, the information conveyed by the sound effects of the echoing footsteps tells the audience that the character has entered the comparative safety of the cathedral. If a narrator had been used to explain what was happening and highlight the panicky thought processes of the character, the scene would have lost its sense of urgency and the audience would have found it dull.

Writing to persuade

Writing for a reading audience

The ideas listed below have been used successfully by students to produce persuasive writing for a reading audience. Look at the list and consider whether there are any ideas that you could try:
- an opinion piece for a magazine
- an advertising campaign
- a leaflet aimed at 18-year-olds to persuade them to give blood for the first time
- a letter to parents of prospective gap-year students

You may have a strong opinion about a topic and feel that you could write an article about it. Many students submit an article for their coursework, but if it has not been crafted using a style model and a clear understanding of the target audience, it can result in writing that feels like an 'essay'. At AS you have to write for a real audience, and essay-type writing does not fulfil this criterion.

This section looks at how writing an article can be used to persuade an audience. However, article writing is not the only, or necessarily the best, choice for your coursework piece. It is used here simply as an example to explain how persuasion can be achieved.

Writing newspaper and magazine feature articles

When many students approach writing to persuade, they have the initial misconception that to be effective they must express their opinion in a strong manner. Actually, the opposite can often be true — a more subtle approach can persuade the reader to re-evaluate his/her ideas. You will encounter this every time you read articles (and opinion pieces), since a good writer will have an agenda that is conveyed to you, the reader. In the most successful writing, the reader absorbs this agenda to the extent that it becomes his/her own opinion. The power of propaganda has been used by political regimes and has been the subject matter of novels, plays and poems.

Think about what you read in terms of persuading or giving an opinion. It could be reviews of recently released films, CDs or computer games as well as more serious opinion pieces commenting on political issues and current affairs. If you cannot think of any newspaper or magazine articles that you have read, then you need to consider carefully whether you should choose to write in this style for a task.

The feature article genre allows you to take an area in which you have a particular interest — and knowledge — and to share it with others. For your writing to be successful you need to provoke interest, use a varied style to retain the interest of the reader and support your opinion with evidence.

AQA (B) Unit 3

Styles of article

Before writing an article, you need to take note of the style in which articles are usually written. It often helps to review a specific example. As you read your chosen example (indeed, as you read anything) ask yourself the following questions:
- Why was it written?
- Who was it written for?
- How is it written?
- How does the writer arouse the interest of the reader?
- How does the writer sustain this interest?
- Is the style successful? If not, why not?
- What other aspects of the writer's style could you either try to use or aim to avoid?

You should consider this set of questions every time you analyse a style model. A key to success is that you understand how professional writers craft their texts, before you begin to write your own.

Before you decide on your own style models, which will reflect your own interests and reading tastes, you may find it useful to analyse the following article, which appeared in the *Daily Telegraph* newspaper in November 2004. The article may appear initially to inform the reader, but when the plight of the sloth bears has been fully explained, the article generates an engagement, to the extent that the reader may be motivated to send a donation to an animal charity. This response is catered for at the end of the passage, with details of the website address and a telephone number. The article was not written as a charity appeal, but the end result is that it works in a similar (and effective) way.

Charities help to rescue India's dancing bears

by Peter Foster (in Agra)

Once they danced for the amusement of Rajput kings and Mughal emperors, but today India's endangered sloth bears must perform for a less rarefied audience — the international tourist.

On the road to Agra, bear handlers wait in dusty dhaba (restaurant) car parks for customers arriving by the busload on the way to the Taj Mahal. There is no shortage of takers.

Each bear has a rope threaded through its roughly pierced snout. A small tug is sufficiently painful to coax the animal onto its hind legs where it sways gently to and fro, as if 'dancing'.

'Would you like to pat him? He won't bite,' demonstrates the handler. 'The children can even ride on his back. Come, quick, "click" a picture with the bear. Only 500 rupees.'

In their excitement — caught up in the novelty perhaps — the punters don't seem to notice the pitiful condition of the bears that work the roadsides, dancing for a living.

On close inspection, the bears' snouts (the rope passes through the roof of the animal's mouth) are visibly raw and bleeding; their toothless gums are foaming and their fur coats, almost black in the wild, are faded brown with malnutrition.

It is only when a healthy bear called Chameli comes to investigate us at the Agra Bear Rescue Facility, 10 miles north of the city, that the contrast becomes really apparent.

When Chameli arrived at the sanctuary her nose was full of maggots, she was carrying worms and was severely malnourished from living on a meagre diet of plain roti (Indian bread). Today she is still wary of the smell of unfamiliar humans, but her snout has healed, her body weight almost doubled and her thick, shaggy coat is once again a lustrous black.

Chameli is one of 57 lucky bears rescued from the roads around Agra in a groundbreaking project that is now set to expand rapidly in order to end a 500-year-old Indian tradition.

With financial assistance from a Sussex-based charity, International Animal Rescue, it is planned to rescue a further 40 bears by Christmas, bringing the total at the 17-acre sanctuary to 100.

The Agra project, in conjunction with an Indian charity Wildlife SOS, is innovative because handlers are being offered generous seed-loans in exchange for their bears.

'This is the first time an animal welfare group has dealt with the social welfare needs of the people as well as the animal welfare needs of the neglected species,' said Alan Knight, the chief executive of IAR, who visited India this week.

Another 80 acres of land given by the Uttar Pradesh state forestry commission will, funds permitting, enable the rescue of 500 more bears within the next 2 years. There are estimated to be 1,000 captive sloth bears in India, with a further 11,000 living wild in Sri Lanka, Burma and the Himalayan belt.

The bears, which can be bought from poachers as cubs for as little as 300 rupees (£3.75), are all owned and trained by members of the nomadic Muslim Kalandar tribe who have no other source of income.

Traditionally the tribe moved from village to village entertaining the people by making the bears lie on their backs, dance, shake hands and nod their heads.

The practice was outlawed in 1972 but has continued largely unchecked.

The sloth bear (*Melursus ursinus*) is preferred because it is small, doesn't hibernate and is 'myrmecophagous' — meaning it eats ants and termites — which gives it its long, attractive, quizzical-looking snout. Under the new rescue scheme every Kalandar who surrenders his bear receives 50,000 rupees (£625) to start up a business. Successes so far include a bicycle repair shop, welding business, vegetable hand carts and rickshaw drivers. A carpet-weaving factory is planned.

In return, the Kalandars must sign a legally binding contract promising not to acquire another bear on pain of arrest, imprisonment and seizure of all assets in order to repay the start-up loan. 'We have to make life bearable, without the bears, if you'll excuse the pun' said Mr Knight, 'although this will obviously costs money — perhaps as much as £700,000 over 2 years.'

One of the Kalandars, Ashiq Miyan, now works at the rescue facility preparing the food for the animals.

He believes that, with the right support, most of his tribe are prepared to give up the bears. 'Since I was 10 years old I would take the bhalus [bears] from village to village with my father. It was our job for the last 300 years, but this is better now,' he said.

'I get the same money [about 4,000 rupees or £50 per month] but now I don't have to run from the police. The bhalus are also happier here.'

International Animal Rescue, **www.iar.org.uk**, 01825 767688

Daily Telegraph, Saturday 13 November 2004

This is an example of a feature article, with a general focus on an animal charity and specific details of the dancing bears. The article was written in Agra, although the charity (International Animal Rescue) is based in the UK. Peter Foster, the journalist, has written in a way that is biased favourably towards the charity. The overall effect of the writing is to persuade, because even though many facts are given, they contribute towards the persuasiveness of the article. International Animal Rescue has been grateful for Foster's unsolicited support, since this article resulted in a large number of people donating money. This has raised funds to buy the land referred to in the article and, consequently, has allowed more bears to be rescued.

When you have read the article, you should consider how it is constructed. You should ask yourself the questions below when reading examples of articles. They provide a framework for analysing your style model.

Why was it written?
We may not know the exact reason, but it is an example of a composite article that newspapers commission freelance writers to produce. It adds interest and variety to the newspaper — newspapers try to be entertaining as well as informative. It was produced for the 'World News' section of the newspaper, which addresses issues from countries around the world. It could be that India had not been considered for some time and the editor wanted to include a topic that reflected a particularly Indian perspective, but this is only speculation.

Who was it written for?
Obviously, it was written for the readership of the *Daily Telegraph*. However, it is not going to engage all readers. Some will read it and be unaffected by it. Others will be interested and feel sorry for the plight of the bears or will be pleased to see a successful initiative that is dealing with the social welfare needs of the owners as well as the animal welfare of the bears. These may be people who have an interest in charitable organisations, or an interest in animal welfare. They may be tourists who have visited India and seen the bears or they may be concerned about environmental issues such as the protection of endangered species.

How is it written? How does the writer arouse the interest of the reader?
The first paragraph offers a contrast between the rarefied role of dancing bears in the past (for the amusement of kings and emperors) and their lives now, with the implication that they are victims of commercialism and even exploitation.

A scene is set (the dhaba car parks) on the coach trips to visit the Taj Mahal, with the inclusion of the words used by the handlers and the excitement of the 'punter'. This negative word, used in connection with horse racing or drinking in a club or pub, is linked with the adjective 'pitiful'. In the next paragraph, the graphic details expand the word 'pitiful'.

The contrast with the healthy bear (Chameli) outlines for the reader what the article is about. The horror (maggots, worms, malnourished) is balanced by Chameli's return to health. However, the abuse she endured has had a long-lasting effect: Chameli will always be wary of the smell of unknown humans.

How does the writer sustain this interest?
Having established this hook into the account, the article gives details of the charity and its work. The details are supported by facts that indicate the poverty of bear handlers: the cheap cost of a poached bear cub (it costs more for one tourist to take a photograph than it does to buy the illegally obtained animal); the cost of setting up a business and their monthly income. The legal (and morally right) stance of the charity is supported by legislation: it is illegal to own dancing bears, although the practice continues unchecked; the owners sign legal contracts to ensure that further bears are not acquired. It is this legal commitment and the awareness that life for the bear handlers must continue to be commercially productive that add authority to the work of the charity.

Is the style successful? If not, why not?
Only you can answer this question, since any article will depend on a personal response. But the style clearly did work for the intended readership, since many donated money to the charity. It must be emphasised that this article was not written by someone whose agenda was to promote the charity. If a more emotive appeal had been made, would it have worked as well on as large a number of people? Possibly not. The promotion of the charity was incidental.

What other aspects of the writer's style could you either try to use or aim to avoid?
This is a well-written article that informs readers about the culture of the nomadic Kalandars in India, details the sensitive role of a UK-based charity and has a 'feel-good' factor about those bears that are rescued. It uses facts and describes the living conditions of both dancing and rescued bears, allowing the reader to see the contrast. It avoids being over-descriptive or heavy-handed or (even worse) bullying the reader.

Hints
- Use language appropriate to what you are writing and who you are writing for.
- Do not use jargon. You cannot assume that the reader has the same background knowledge as you do.
- Read examples from the various sources you are interested in using as a style model, and familiarise yourself with the style. A conversational tone may be appropriate for one article but inappropriate for another.
- Consider carefully whether people really want to read about your subject. You may find it helpful to try out an idea on your family and friends first.
- Avoid a patronising tone. Assuming too little knowledge can be as off-putting for the reader as assuming too much.
- Always use a short word in preference to a longer one, provided it is equally accurate. A reader of a short article will not want to be reaching for a dictionary.
- Do not embroider your prose. Write in an imaginative way but not at the expense of presenting the facts.
- Write in a lively way. You can afford to be less formal in an article than in a textbook, for example. Convey your enthusiasm. Avoid passive, formal language such as: 'It is believed that' or 'One is required to'.

- Check your work by reading aloud for 'readability'. Can you read it with ease? Can you eliminate any non-essential words?
- You can include photographs or illustrations as appropriate, but do not waste time trying to place the text in newspaper-style columns unless you have the necessary IT skills.

Finding the facts

You may wish to consider how writers can appear so knowledgeable about their subjects. Most non-fiction refers to outside sources. A shorter piece of writing, such as an article, may require only minimal research, but it may be necessary to check facts (remember that a persuasive text acquires credibility by the judicious use of facts).

Sources that can be used include:
- encyclopaedias
- newspapers
- art galleries
- catalogues
- magazines
- museums
- specialised textbooks
- local libraries

However, for many people, a key source of research is the internet. It is readily accessible and a useful tool, but it comes with an official warning from the examination board:

Unfair practice
Candidates must not take part in any unfair practice in the preparation of coursework to be submitted for assessment, and must understand that to present material copied directly (from any source) without acknowledgement will be regarded as deliberate deception.

What about persuasion?

If you are writing articles to persuade, you need to select an appropriate reading audience, address the audience in a tone that replicates style models, and present an opinion in a way that influences the reader. Subtlety will achieve a greater level of success than an article that uses a prescribed number of rhetorical devices and a tone that is the metaphorical equivalent of shouting in the middle of normal speech.

At GCSE you learned about rhetorical devices (probably when delivering a speech) that can be used to sway the emotions of an audience. It is important to remember that a reader is more distant from the writer, and therefore the persuasion needs to be more restrained. It is still possible to use emotional appeal. You can:
- ask the opinion of the reader
- compliment the reader
- imply that something will occur
- criticise the point of view of those who disagree
- use inclusive pronouns such as 'we' or 'our'
- encourage the readership to take action
- end in a powerful or thought-provoking manner

You can also use many features of language — for example, you can:
- use metaphorical/descriptive language
- quote specific examples
- employ balanced phrases
- juxtapose opposites
- list (often in threes), building up to a climax
- pose questions
- use repetition
- choose emotive language

All these techniques come with a warning — do not overuse them or labour your opinion.

Writing for a listening audience

The following ideas have been used successfully by students to produce persuasive writing for a listening audience. Consider whether there are any ideas that you could try:
- a radio charity appeal
- a television programme on divorce
- an advertising campaign (on television or radio) for a specific product
- a (topical or moral) talk for a school assembly

If you choose to write a radio advertisement, either as a radio charity appeal or an advertising campaign, you must remember the restriction on the number of words. Radio and television advertisements last between 30 and 40 seconds, which is approximately 150–200 words.

The following section considers the skills you will need to script a radio charity appeal. It has been chosen to show you how persuasion can be used for a listening audience. However, the radio charity appeal is not the only, or the best, choice.

Writing a radio charity appeal

You may find it useful to refer to the section in 'Writing to entertain' which looks at writing radio drama (pp. 24–25).

If you are writing a radio advertisement to persuade, there are ten commandments that you should obey:
(1) Use music or sound effects.
(2) Have a variety of voices — but no more than three.
(3) Make simple statements rather than long, complex ones.
(4) Use repetition or recap, especially for contact details or key information.
(5) The duration should be 30–40 seconds.
(6) Convey emotion and/or enthusiasm.
(7) Target the campaign to your listening audience — for example, local radio, Classic FM, Talk Sport etc.

AQA (B) Unit 3

(8) Use a catch phrase or slogan.
(9) Address the audience.
(10) End on an upbeat/uplifting note.

You may not need to use all ten commandments, but you must consider whether you have included a sufficient number for your radio advertisement (or charity appeal) to work.

You may have been moved, for example, by the plight of the sloth bears about in the *Daily Telegraph* article and decide to produce a radio appeal that could be used for fundraising purposes.

Your radio appeal could take the following form:

FX Indian dance music and crowd sounds

NARRATOR 1: I'm on a guided tour of northern India. On our visit to the Taj Mahal we're approaching Agra on the road from Delhi. I've just witnessed the ghastly sight of a bear being dragged by a rope that was threaded through his nose. He was being pulled violently up on to the back of a lorry.

NARRATOR 2: He was one of India's dancing bears. They perform for tourists; a small tug on the rope that pierces their nose is painful enough to make them rise on to their hind legs to dance. Their teeth have been knocked out and their claws removed to make them easier to handle.

FX hand bell rings

HANDLER: Would you like to pat him? He won't bite. Come, quick, click a picture with the bear.

NARRATOR 2: International Animal Rescue has a bear sanctuary at Agra, which provides a caring home for dancing bears that have been rescued from the streets of India.

FX Indian dance music

When they arrive their muzzles are often dripping with pus and blood.

FX loud purring noise

NARRATOR 2: That's the noise that they make when they're treated with loving care and kindness. That bear has just eaten his favourite meal of porridge, honey and seeds.

End FX loud purring noise

They're learning to live freely again.

NARRATOR 2: International Animal Rescue needs your help to continue its work, saving these bears. Find out about our charity at www.iar.org.uk. Or telephone 01825 767688. It is our dream to rescue all of India's dancing bears. And with your help, we can realise that dream. International Animal Rescue at www.iar.org.uk. Or telephone 01825 767688.

The appeal starts (as the article did) with a description of a typical scene encountered by tourists. This serves the purpose of persuasion for the 'tourist' on the coach to have more perception than was apparent in the *Daily Telegraph* article. Local colour is added by using the handler's voice to capture the scene described in the article. The same contrasting treatment and condition of the bears in the streets and in the sanctuary is presented, supported by sound effects that convey the contentment of the bears — the narrator has to explain to the listening audience exactly what the sound that they were hearing is. There is the same descriptive use of adjectives as in the original article (*small, caring, loving*) and adverbs (*ghastly, violently*). Halfway through the appeal, the charity's name is introduced, and then reinforced by repetition. The website address and telephone number are repeated, leaving a short space to allow the listener to make a note of the details, either mentally or literally.

The advantage of using a charity to present a radio appeal is that there will be support material, either on the internet or from publications. As long as you choose a charitable trust that interests you, you will be engaged in your writing and the necessary research. However, it is important that you ensure that what you write is original and uses the source material only as a resource.

Remember that this is only the beginning of the process of learning how to write for radio, and you will need to develop your skills by listening to radio, particularly Radio 4, which offers a wide variety of scripted programmes. You should also experiment with more demanding radio tasks than advertisements if you want to achieve a high level of success. The BBC Radio 4 website can be used to access information about radio programmes, including scripts, at **www.bbc.co.uk/radio4/index.shtml?logo**

Writing to inform

Writing for a reading audience

This is the category that often produces the best (and most imaginative) writing, particularly if you write from personal experience. The scope of topics and the way in which they can be presented are wide. The following ideas have been used successfully by students to produce informative writing for a reading audience:
- an AS induction booklet

AQA (B) Unit 3

- children's non-fiction writing
- an autobiography
- travel writing — using school trips abroad to China, Russia, San Francisco and Romania (and less exotic places)
- an art exhibition information pack
- museum booklets
- careers guidelines

The following section looks at writing to inform children about the Great Fire of London. It offers a useful introduction to writing for a specific audience, as it allows you to consider the sorts of questions that you must always ask yourself about an audience. Again, writing about the Great Fire of London is only an example from the many that you could choose.

Writing for children

The *Anthology* for Unit 1 of the English Language and Literature specification provides a useful resource. It contains a historical written source that can be used to teach history to children in primary schools, at Key Stage 1 and Key Stage 2.

The Great Fire of London is an important event in English history. It raged from 2 September 1666 for 5 days and the destruction can be compared only with that of the Second World War blitz on cities in the UK. In the days of the Great Fire of London, there was no separate 'central business district' as there is today — central London was where many people lived, so the impact was much the same as the blitz in the 1940s.

Samuel Pepys was not only a diarist but also a government official (he was Secretary for the Navy) and he portrays the drama of the fire in a simple and compelling way. The National Curriculum requires that children should hear the words of an eyewitness to an event, and Pepys's diaries present us with such a source.

If you intend to write for children for either of your coursework texts, you must ask yourself:
- What is the age/ability/interest of the children I am writing for?
- What do children read/understand/enjoy?
- What are the demands of writing for this audience?
- What contact do I have with pupils or teachers?

Research and audience testing are essential — and you should ask yourself these questions for all audiences.

Writing to inform for a younger age group can be an ideal option, since the information researched has to be edited and modified for the target audience and this means that there is more opportunity to write something original. Most importantly, it avoids the issue of an informative text being heavily dependent on the source material, which reduces the mark that you can be awarded for the text.

Since the focus for this particular task is on school children, the first stage in the writing process is to look at what pupils in Key Stages 1 and 2 have to read as part of the National Curriculum. Documents on the National Curriculum state that children have to:
- read non-fiction and non-literary texts for information — including diaries, autobiographies, biographies and letters
- use reference materials such as encyclopaedias and textbooks
- read challenging and demanding subject matter

The National Curriculum also states which topics children must study. This can provide a useful starting point for you as a writer, since there may be topics on this list about which you have specialist knowledge, for example:
- **history** — Ancient Egyptians, Romans, Anglo-Saxons, Vikings, wives of Henry VIII, Industrial Revolution, Victorian Britain, Second World War, Britain since 1948, famous people
- **science** — forces, electricity, circuits and conductors, magnets and springs, light and shadow, friction, planets
- **biology** — plant life, life cycles, human body, habitats
- **geography** — weather around the world, local environmental issues, water, rivers, coast, villages in India
- **religion** — different faiths and beliefs
- **design technology** — materials and their properties, musical instruments, money containers, torches
- **current affairs** — any topic in the news

Skills involved in writing to inform for children

This section assumes that you are working from the Samuel Pepys source material.

First, you need to decide if you are writing for Key Stage 1 pupils (probably the older end of the age range at 6–7 years old) or for Key Stage 2 pupils. This will affect what you write in a number of ways:
- The amount of text that you write — although you will need to give a more general overview than lots of details for both key stages, you will need to give more information for Key Stage 2.
- Vocabulary used — you will not use expressions such as 'flames had *consumed...*' or 'into the *neighbouring* Thames Street' for Key Stage 1.
- Sentence structure — when writing for Key Stage 1, this will need to be uncomplicated, with a greater use of simple and compound sentences than for Key Stage 2. You should make comparisons, such as 'the fire was greater than...' to clarify details.

When writing for children you should also bear in mind the following points:
- Tone — you need to inform, without being too inaccessible and 'learned' or being condescending and 'talking down' to the reader.
- Specialist language — avoid using specialist language. If you do, explain it in a glossary or in the text.
- You could choose to use a personal or impersonal approach. It may be appropriate to use the perspective of a child during the time of the Great Fire of London.

AQA (B) Unit 3

- You can use techniques or devices to aid children's understanding:
  - pictures/engravings with explanatory captions
  - cartoon/graphic sketches
  - key facts in bullet points or boxes
  - 'fascinating facts'
  - headings and subheadings
  - breaking up the text
  - clear typeface and fonts

Remember that your coursework is assessed on the text that is written, not on the graphics or coloured pictures. You do not need to spend time importing these into the text. A box with an indication of contents is sufficient. For example:

Picture of Samuel Pepys	A map of London as it looked before the fire

Source material: the Great Fire of London, 1666

Remind yourself of the first paragraph of the eyewitness account written in 1666 by Samuel Pepys (Text 22 in the *Anthology* for Unit 1). He was born in London in 1633, educated at Cambridge and became one of the most important civil servants of his age. Between 1660 and 1669 he kept a diary. This extract describes the start of the Great Fire of London. Sarah is a junior maid in Pepys's household; Betty Michell is a friend of Pepys.

Sample answer — a textbook account for Key Stage 1

At three o'clock in the morning Jane, the servant of Samuel Pepys, woke him up. She had seen a fire and wanted to tell him. He put on his dressing gown and had a look. It was a long way away, so he went back to bed.

At seven o'clock he got up and got dressed. Then he went with the son of one of his friends to have a look at the fire. Lots of houses were burning. He was very worried because some of his friends lived in that area. He went to see the person in charge of the Tower of London who told him that the fire had started in a baker's house in Pudding Lane. Lots of houses nearby had already been burnt down.

He went down to the river and got on a boat, to look more closely. Nobody was trying to put the fire out. Instead, they stayed in their own homes as long as they could. When the fire got too close, they threw what they owned to the nearby boats in the river.

Sample answer — a textbook account for Key Stage 2

At three o'clock in the morning on Sunday 2 September 1666 Jane, the maid of Samuel Pepys, woke him up. She had been preparing for a feast the following day and had seen a great fire in the city. Samuel Pepys got up, put on his dressing gown and looked out of the window to see the fire. It seemed to be a long way away and he was not concerned that there would be any immediate danger. So he returned to bed and went back to sleep.

At about seven o'clock Pepys got up, dressed himself and looked out of the window again. The fire was still a long way away but seemed to be larger than when he had seen it early in the morning. Jane told him that she heard that over 300 houses had been burnt down and that the whole of Fish Street was alight.

Samuel Pepys walked to the Tower of London to get a better view from one of the high points. Sir J. Robinson's little son went with him to see the extent of the fire. Samuel Pepys was concerned because one of his friends and one of the maids lived in that area of London. He was very worried about what he had seen and went to speak to the Lieutenant of the Tower, who explained that the fire had started in the King's baker's house in Pudding Lane and had burned down St Magnes church and most of Fish Street. He went down to the river Thames and got a boat and sailed through the bridge to look at the huge fire. His friend's house had already been burnt down and the fire extended as far as the steel yard. Everybody was trying to get their goods to safety and throwing them into boats in the river. Poor people stayed in their houses as long as they could until the fire reached them. Then they rushed into boats or clambered down the steps by the waterside to escape. Even the pigeons did not want to leave their houses, but hovered around the windows and balconies until they burnt their wings and fell down.

Differences between the Key Stage 1 and Key Stage 2 sample answers

The most obvious difference between the two sample answers is the word count. The text for Key Stage 1 is about 180 words long; the text for Key Stage 2 is double that at 360 words. This means that the accounts vary in the amount of detail given. Consider how much more detail there is in the Key Stage 2 text:

- Jane is preparing a feast
- a detailed description of Pepys's initial view of the fire
- rumours of what Jane has heard
- the initial visit to the Tower of London
- information about the child
- information about Michell's and Sarah's houses
- destruction of St Magnes church and the steel yard
- the river is named as the Thames (Key Stage 2 children are expected to know this river)
- Michell's house has been destroyed
- considerable detail about how the poor reacted, ending with the reference to the pigeons — this description will engage children

The details used in the Key Stage 2 text are intended to increase the children's understanding of the event and to clarify the account. They reflect the pupils' increased understanding of people and events.

Linguistically, the lexis used in the Key Stage 1 version has only one three-syllable word (nobody), and the rest of the lexis is comprised of one- and two-syllable words. There is lexical repetition (lots of houses...lots of houses; got up...got dressed). Most of the verbs are past tense without auxiliary verbs — the exceptions are 'He was worried', 'fire had started', and 'nobody was trying'. There is only one passive verb usage ('had been burnt down').

In contrast, the Key Stage 2 text varies the lexis, with 11 polysyllabic words, and much lexical variety ('over 300 houses'; 'he got up, dressed himself'). There is also a more complex sentence structure — note the sentence beginning 'He was very worried...Fish Street', which has four clauses (many other sentences have three clauses).

Sources
This section ends with details about sources that you can use when writing to inform. You will be more successful in writing to inform if you have a clear idea of who you are writing for and how you will need to adapt the source material. You can use:
- history dictionaries
- encyclopaedias
- atlases and map books
- historical maps
- topic-based information books
- textbooks
- Study Unit text (written specifically for the National Curriculum)
- fact sheets
- non-fiction picture books
- museum exhibitions
- collections of photographs in local history section of libraries
- CD-ROMs
- archive newspapers
- the internet

Writing for a listening audience

The following ideas have been used successfully by students to produce informative writing for a listening audience:
- a family history DVD
- a sight and sound presentation in a local art gallery
- a museum audio guide
- a local history talk on your own town
- radio documentaries

You may notice that several of these ideas relate to the expertise of students in their own family, local or subject knowledge.

Samuel Pepys's diary extract, which was used in the previous section for writing for a reading audience, could also be developed for a listening audience, in the form of a television performance. This could be a re-enactment of the event for children's television, for example.

The television script below was chosen to show how you can access source information in the same way whether you choose to write for a reading audience or a listening audience — the initial research is the same. The key to success is in the scripting of the information for a specific television (or radio) audience.

The Great Fire of London — television script

Scene 1

View of bedroom door. Jane knocking frantically.

JANE: Mr Pepys, Mr Pepys, Mr Pepys.

Change view to inside the room. Samuel Pepys gets up, puts on dressing gown and answers the door.

PEPYS: What on earth is the matter?

JANE: Master, there's a big fire in the distance. I can just see it from my bedroom window.

Change view to servants' staircase. Pepys follows Jane up narrow staircase to her bedroom window. Both go to window and peer out.

PEPYS: It's a long way off, Jane. It looks as if it's the far side of Marke Lane to me.

What time is it?

JANE: It's three in the morning, sir. We were just finishing the preparations for today's feast.

PEPYS: Well, I think we can all go to bed now and see what it looks like in the morning. It doesn't look particularly dangerous.

Scene 2

Church clock chimes. View of clock face at seven o'clock seen through a window. Camera moves back to show Pepys standing at window in nightshirt, looking at the clock and rising black smoke behind it.

PEPYS: (Calling.) Jane, bring me some water. (Stretching, moving to dresser.)

Scene 3

Jane talking to Watch at the street door.
Cut to Jane knocking on Pepys's bedroom door and entering carrying a pitcher. She pours water into the basin on the dresser.

JANE: I've been talking to the Watch. He says that over 300 houses have burnt down in the fire that we saw. He says it's burning down all Fish Street by London Bridge.

PEPYS:	Right. I'll get dressed and have a look.

Scene 4

Cut to downstairs as Pepys is fully dressed and holding hat and cape.

JANE:	Young master Robinson is awake. He wants to know if he can go with you, sir.
PEPYS:	If he can be ready in 5 minutes he can come.
JANE:	He will be.

Scene 5

Street scene. Pepys and child are walking together.

PEPYS:	We'll go to the Tower to get a better view of the fire.

Scene 6

Cut to high point of Tower. The two stand looking at the city below them.

CHILD:	Look, sir. All the houses at the end of the bridge are on fire!
PEPYS:	Oh no! That's where Betty Michell lives. And little Sarah the maid.
	I need to go and speak to the Lieutenant of the Tower.

Scene 7

Location within Tower of London. Impression of chaos with people hurrying past.

LIEUTENANT:	Sad day, Mr Pepys. From the information I've received the fire began in the King's baker's house in Pudding Lane. It's burned down St Magnes church and most of Fish Street already.
PEPYS:	We need to take a closer look. I'll take a boat up the river to see the damage at first hand. I'll be back shortly, sir, to give you further report.

Scene 8

Location on Thames pier steps.

PEPYS:	Boatman.
BOATMAN:	'Tis Mr Pepys.
PEPYS:	I need to go up the river to view the extent of the fire.
BOATMAN:	It's very dangerous, sir. I'll have to charge you a shilling.
PEPYS:	*(Paying.)* Make haste, man.

BOATMAN: Aye, sir.

Scene 9

Location on river. Impression given that they have been viewing the scene in silence for some time.

PEPYS: *(Regretful tone.)* I do believe Betty's house has burnt down. All the houses as far as the Old Swan are burnt away. And still the fire is spreading — at an ever-increasing rate.

BOATMAN: It will soon be as far as the steel yard.

CHILD: Look, Mr Pepys. All the rich people are trying to save their goods by throwing them to the boats in the river.

PEPYS: You're right, boy. But it's the poor I'm concerned about. Why do they stop in their houses until the fire gets to the door? And then they have to dash down the stairs. Are they so fearful of losing their few possessions that they put their own lives at risk?

Scene 10

Location back at the tower. Pepys talking to harassed-looking lieutenant. Impression given that the report has repeated what has already been said in the boat and this is Pepys's summative comment.

LIEUTENANT: ...And?

PEPYS: No one seems to be trying to put the fire out.

Notes on writing a television script
- The reference at the end of one scene can explain the location of the following scene — for example, the transition from Scene 5 to Scene 6.
- Characters must be introduced to the audience — for example, Mr Pepys is called by name in the opening sequence of Scene 1. His position of power is made evident by three different modes of address in that same scene: 'Mr', 'Master' and 'Sir'. Jane is also referred to by name later in that same scene, and she introduces the child in Scene 4.
- There are relatively few characters — the play is not cluttered with other servants or with Pepys's family members.
- There is a variety of scenes to interest the viewers.
- In television, the visual picture conveys information to the audience. For example, in Scene 2, the visuals of the clock face, the black smoke and Pepys in his night-shirt let the audience know that it is seven o'clock in the morning and that the fire is still burning.

The techniques used in radio drama (see pp. 24–25) are also relevant to scripting television drama.

Writing to advise/instruct

Writing for a reading audience

Students often find it most difficult to generate ideas when writing to advise or instruct, so it may be helpful to consider examples of successful writing. Many of the ideas below could be used for either a reading or a listening audience:

- a GNVQ Health and Childcare student instructs families and carers of newborn babies about preventing cot deaths
- advice to parents before buying their child a horse
- revision for the theory part of the driving test
- advice on the appropriate selection of a scooter for 16-year-olds
- a series of web pages on study skills for GCSE students
- advice on buying your first guitar

You need to have some expertise that means you can advise or instruct and, as always, it is best to select a subject that you know about. However, it can be useful to look at an example of a writing style that has its own codes and conventions.

The following activity has been chosen because most students are familiar with websites. It is also realistic to expect that if someone wanted advice or instructions, then they may access it through a search engine rather than using more traditional methods, such as audio tapes, booklets or manuals.

Writing for websites

The purpose of this first section is to alert you to some of the considerations and restrictions to be borne in mind when writing for websites:

- The standard amount of text per page is 256 words. If images/graphics are used, the amount of text will be reduced proportionally.
- Images/graphics help the web page to look user-friendly
- The pages should be (as much as possible) about doing things (rather than reading) and looking at things other than text — since reading large amounts of text online can be tedious.
- It is better to hand control over to the users and ask them to press a button — whether this reveals further information or takes them on to the next page.
- A web page can include:
  - multiple-choice options — choose from possible answers by clicking in the appropriate box
  - quiz-type activities — for example, true/false
  - icons that can be clicked on to reveal text
  - run-on animation — either by clicking on various points on the picture to see different effects or which runs continuously
  - text that can be linked to audio script

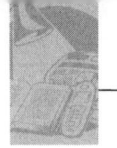

- drag-and-drop can be used for labelling on diagrams, filling in missing words in sentences etc.
- In general, the less you put on any one web page, the better it works. You can use organisational features such as:
  - bullet points
  - numbering
  - tables
  - short, clearly labelled sections
  - questions

The next section contains text that has been written as a design for three web pages to be accessed by AS students wanting to know how to write to advise/instruct. These three texts are not actual web pages, and you are not expected to set up your own website. The text is what you would submit as an example of a web-page design. Your teacher, and the moderator, will assess your text on the basis of how successfully it would work as a real web page.

Italics are used to convey information to the web-page designer and would not be seen on the final web page.

Web page 1
What do people use for instructions or advice? Do they use:

The following list shown as icons indicated for user to click on to reveal the text
- internet and computer instruction and advice?   *A computer screen*
- advisory booklets?   *A book with question mark*
- interactive CD-ROM?   *A CD*
- advice in the form of an audio cassette?   *A stereo player*
- a series of posters?   *A poster*
- a beginner's guide?   *A face with question marks above it*
- the script for a cassette/broadcast programme?   *A scroll*

In the space below, write down any other ideas you have for writing that could advise or instruct. Think of everything you read, listen to or watch that instructs or advises you. Choose a topic in which you have experience and skill.

Space for user to type in other ideas here

NEXT *Click for new page*

Web page 2
You may wonder why you are advised to choose an area in which you have experience or skills when thinking of ideas. It is because this always produces the best writing. For example, if you are a volunteer helper or a part-time worker, you will know what others need to know and what is not covered in professionally published texts.

AQA (B) Unit 3

> Be realistic. It is impossible to learn to swim with an instruction book in one hand.
>
> *Insert illustration of someone swimming that becomes an animation when user clicks on it*
>
> Learning how to play the piano would be far too much to write about, but a small section on counting and rhythm practice would be appropriate.
>
> *Insert illustration of piano which plays musical rhythm clip when user clicks on it*
>
> NEXT *Click for new page*

> **Web page 3**
> The experience does not have to be your own.
>
> One student had a brother who was away at university. He knew that his brother managed on very little money — even with a priority of socialising! He found out what strategies his brother had used, and they became
>
> 'The only guide to surviving university'. *Presented in colour as the title of the student's text*
>
> Advice covered 'nights out' *Click here* **The key to being a good student is to cut down on everything except beer; always try and make a friend behind the bar — this makes your nights out even cheaper.**
>
> and
>
> 'top money-saving tips' *Click here* **If you pick a uni close to home you can easily pop home at weekends — for the laundry service and free food in the fridge and cupboards; take two duvets and sleep in a balaclava, a fleece jacket and bed socks — heating is expensive.**
>
> *Use student voices for the italic bold — the text is not needed*

Notes on writing for websites
You will have noticed a number of features in the example above:
- The text is relatively short (approximately 440 words) — this is appropriate for an introduction.
- There are three pages indicated on the website, since there is a relatively small amount of text alongside the graphics.
- A range of activities is included:
    - icons to reveal text
    - user to type in text
    - click for new page
    - animation
    - audio links

- The special effects are indicated in text form. It is not necessary to spend time creating the graphics. Your work is assessed by how a web-page writer would visualise what you have indicated in your text.

Even if you are writing for a less traditional medium, such as a website, you need to use language appropriate for writing that advises or instructs. The language features in the list below could be used whenever you attempt to instruct or advise your audience:
- imperative sentences — tell the audience through direct commands
- friendly tone — even though you are directing the audience, do it in a pleasant manner
- information that will explain the instruction
- vocabulary specific to the subject matter
- jargon (where appropriate) which is explained
- sequential writing — number your points or use words like first, second, etc.
- graphology features such as bullet points, brackets, variety of fonts, headings and subheadings, illustrations
- write as if answering an unspoken question
- questions — you can employ a question and answer format (Q & A), or a frequently asked questions section (FAQ)
- examples and explanations
- tips/handy hints

Writing for a listening audience

Some of the ideas suggested for reading audiences are particularly appropriate for writing for a listening audience:
- revision for the theory part of the driving test — as audio tape
- a GNVQ Health and Childcare student instructs families and carers of newborn babies about preventing cot deaths — as a talk

Other ideas include:
- how to start tracing family history roots — as a television script
- an excerpt from the radio programme 'Does he take sugar?' called 'Vision to succeed'

One of the best tips to follow when planning to script your instructions or advice for a listening audience is to envisage the audience in front of you — talk out loud as though the audience were real.

Giving a talk, a potentially difficult scripting task, has been chosen as an example of writing for a listening audience. You must remember that it is not the only, or the best, option available.

Because you are scripting a talk, and not chatting with friends, you must maintain a level of formality. The talk has to be planned, it has to address and engage the target audience and it needs to use some degree of audience participation to ensure that it succeeds in its instructions or advice.

To write a successful talk you will need to:
- Give the talk a structure. A clearly defined beginning, middle and end are essential. Do not try to include too much — deliver one key message.
- Use visual aids to demonstrate or illustrate the point being made. Keep them simple and appropriate. For an instructive talk it is not a cliché to have a 'Here's one I made earlier' approach, as long as you can demonstrate the process in the real time of the talk.
- Be creative in your use of language — try to put across your personality.
- Interact with your audience. Think about who you are talking to and aim to engage them. Ensure that you do not say anything that could be considered offensive or condescending.

The next section is an extract from a talk that gives advice about writing a commentary for coursework. It was delivered by an A2 student to AS students and was quite formal, since the talk was given in a lecture room. The student has followed the advice listed above.

How to comment on your own writing

In order to prepare for the commentary, you have to learn how to comment on your own writing. I found that I was able to do this because I did not think of it as an add-on extra. All the decisions that I made, and which you will have made in your own writing, are part of the process of learning how to improve your writing. You will need to record those decisions since they will improve your skills of writing a commentary.

Commenting on your own writing can be linked to the acquisition of any skill. When starting something new, you have to learn the theory and principles underpinning that skill. On a practical level, when I applied for a provisional driving licence, I was informed that I would have to take (and pass) a theory test before I could apply for my practical test. Later on, my first lesson with the driving instructor did not start with me immediately driving the car. What everyone wants, and what I wanted, was to drive, but the instructor had to spend some time in that first lesson telling me about the mechanical operation of the car.

It is like that with the coursework folder. Knowing how English works, in terms of grammar, punctuation and structure of language, is an essential part of understanding the theory of how to write. The problem is that this alone does not help you to write well.

You may remember the sort of 'essays' that we were given when we were at school — such as:

OHT: ⬚ BESIDE THE RIVER ⬚

Or

OHT: ⬚ I shall never forget that day ⬚   (leave OHT displayed)

An essay title is one of the ways of getting us, as students, to write, but it lacks originality. And I remember that I often wrote them without any interest. It was homework. And it didn't engage me. But I became interested when I found out about the theory behind how we tell stories, and discovered that I could analyse what I'd written.

The linguist William Labov used the fact that we were familiar with the technique of narration to research how we structure our stories. He developed the idea that people tell stories in a recognisably similar way and that they narrate events in a predictable pattern. In order to encourage story telling, he asked his subjects this following question:

OHT: ⬚ Have you ever been in a situation where you were in serious danger of being killed? ⬚

Labov reasoned that a question like this would encourage a dramatic response and the speaker would be emotionally involved. Which is exactly why teachers set essays such as: 'I shall never forget that day'. *(Remove OHT)* In fact, if each of you was asked the same question, then I guess you may have a story to tell.

Labov came up with this model for story telling:

OHT *(of six terms only — explanation to be given)*

- Abstract
- Orientation
- Complicating action
- Resolution
- Coda
- Evaluation

(in notes)
- abstract — a brief explanation of what the story is about
- orientation — the who, what, when and where of the story
- complicating action — the 'what happened then?' of the story
- resolution — the 'what finally happened?' of the story; a conclusion is reached
- coda — the story ends and a connection is made to the present situation
- evaluation — at various intervals running through the story the storyteller makes additional comments and gestures to highlight how the story is interesting

Understanding how we structure our stories, particularly when they are narratives, can help us to analyse our writing.

But does it improve it? No, probably not.

Sometimes you may be given a stimulus like this:

OHT:
> Photograph of footprints in the sand

What does that stimulate you to write? Try it now. Think about ideas, words, phrases, perhaps questions that come to mind when looking at that picture. (*2 minutes*)

What was the outcome? (*Ask audience if one or two would like to share their ideas.*)

It could have produced some excellent ideas. It may have made you think of the start of your own story — or maybe not!

The reason for this is that there are a number of ingredients needed to produce effective writing. And these are what you will have to work at. If you spend time thinking about these ingredients, then you have started the process of commenting on your own writing.

Notes on writing a talk
- This talk has a structure — in this extract we see the clearly defined beginning.
- Visual aids are used in the form of overhead transparencies (OHTs) of questions, statements and photographs.
- The text is written as if answering unspoken questions that the audience may be thinking about. Examples are given that may relate to their own experiences (GCSE essays and preparation for the practical section of the driving test) and explanations are given (of Labov's technical terms).
- The audience is actively involved rather than sitting passively the whole time; questions are asked and a task is given that has to be completed in a specified time (responding to a photograph stimulus).
- Techniques are used to give advice or instructions, including the use of information that explains how to start evaluating texts. For example, questions are posed, bullet points on the OHT are explained. There is also a logical sequence starting with memories of school essays and leading up to AS.
- The vocabulary is specific to the subject matter (linguistic terms and Labov's storytelling model).
- There is an attempt to lead the audience to the first stage of commentary writing ('If you spend time thinking about these ingredients, then you have started the process of commenting on your own writing').

The most important thing to remember if you choose to script a talk is that you must practise by delivering the talk to a real audience. This means that you will know whether:
- the talk works
- it is right for the audience
- it can be read aloud

Commentary writing

It is important to put commentary writing into a real-life context. The requirement to write a commentary for each text is not intended to be simply an academic exercise but one that allows you, as the writer, to explain your intentions and the process that you went through to produce your texts.

The process of drafting and redrafting is one that every writer undertakes, whether it is personal notes with some text crossed out or a more formal editing because someone else will read your work. Redrafting does not take place just in education. Commercial companies redraft the wording on products, and advertisers update successful advertising campaigns to make them feel more current. If you look at text written even a few years ago it can seem dated. Only 2 years ago the word 'iPod' would not be understood.

It is useful to look at how the commentary is marked. It is given a mark out of 30, covering your response to both of your texts. You can write either one commentary of 1,000–1,500 words, covering both of your texts, or two separate commentaries, each between 500 and 700 words, dealing with the reading text and then the listening text. Most students do better by writing two separate commentaries.

Guidelines for writing the commentary

These are general guidelines on what to include in your commentary and should not be viewed as a compulsory checklist. Not all of the points will necessarily be appropriate for the texts that you produce.

- Introduction:
  - Genre — you should show awareness of conventions and characteristics.
  - Context — you should indicate where the piece would be published/performed and outline features of a relevant style model that should be emulated.
  - Target audience — the best writing has a clear focus on audience; this can be specific to interests groups or readership rather than an age group.
  - Purpose — you should clarify the primary purpose of your text, although it is inevitable that secondary purposes will be an integral part of any text.
- Features of your style model and identification of these features within the text or reference (with specific details) to research that has been undertaken:
  - It is good practice to show how the piece replicates or improves an admired/disliked style model.
  - The use of a style model applies particularly to the writing of children's stories, magazine articles and journalism.
- Focus on redrafting and the decision-making process regarding the following features:

- Language use — it is important to discuss the language choices you made and their effects.
- Tone/voice — how have you captured a voice/the tone that the target audience can relate to?
- Structure/organisation — you should use specific examples. An economical method is to number the pages of each draft, so that in your commentary you can make references to see Draft 1 page 3, for example.
- Audience response — you should comment on target audience reactions and any changes you made in response.

Points to remember

- The commentary should be an integral part of the crafting process and not an afterthought attached to purposeful writing.
- The best commentaries are those in which candidates have responded thoughtfully to their own texts without following a rigid outline.
- Avoid descriptive commentaries that merely identify what is in the text.
- Ensure that the commentary is analytical and linguistic rather than anecdotal.
- A linguistic analysis highlights significant features and does not give a running commentary on every sentence or go through a 'language checklist'.

If you follow the guidelines above, then your commentary will be able to achieve the highest marks.

In the Student Coursework section, there are examples of two A-grade commentaries. You can see what the students have written for their texts (and read their commentaries), with comments from a moderator.

Your teachers may give you guidelines on how to write your commentary. The two sections below are examples of guidelines given by teachers to their students. Both these examples are helpful guidance for writing your commentary. However, the key point to remember is that neither of these examples is a formula for writing a commentary.

Example 1 Writing a commentary

Your commentary must refer to:
- choices of vocabulary and syntactic structures
- styles of writing
- overall structure and organisation of the text
- changes made during drafting and redrafting

You should include an introduction that clearly states the purpose, audience and context for your text.

You could include the following points in your commentary:

Choices of vocabulary and syntactic structures
- lexis — choice of words
  - modern/Latinate
  - standard English/colloquial
  - formal/informal
  - semantic field
- syntax — sentence structure
- simple/compound/complex
- complete/grammatical/broken
- interrogative/declarative/imperative
- elliptical utterances (following pattern of natural speech)

Styles of writing
- narrative voice
- poetic/literary devices
- rhetorical features
- tense
- formal/informal
- use of a style model — it is good practice to refer to a style model, as it gives you the opportunity to write about language features and refer to your own language choices in the light of your model

Overall structure and organisation of the text
- chronological
- narrative structure
- stages of an argument
- opening/intro/hook
- ending/conclusion/upbeat note
- cohesion
- graphological features

Changes made during drafting and redrafting
- significant changes and developments
- what the changes you made were
- the effect of the changes

Avoid saying 'I altered the spelling and grammar' or 'I didn't make any changes because it was perfect' — or similar comments.

Other points you could discuss
- audience response to your work — aim to trial your text on the appropriate audience
- discourse — the relationship established between writer/reader or speaker/listener

AQA (B) Unit 3

> You must include detailed comments on your language choices. Quote from your own writing and comment on your quotations, explaining the effects of the language you have used.

Example 2 Commentary-writing checklist

Look at the following chart and make sure that your commentary has answered these questions. You might find it useful to jot down notes about your own text as you go through the checklist, which will act as an aid to your memory when you write up your notes.

Question	Notes
Did you need to do any research, background reading or interviews? Give details and include hard copies.	
What style, author or format have you modelled your writing on?	
How did you establish a clear purpose for your text? (Remember that your two texts must have different primary purposes.)	
Who is the audience for your text?	
How did you adapt the following features to address this audience? • lexis • tone • level of formality Give specific examples to illustrate this.	
What signposts (as a means of guidance or indication) have you used to ensure an effective structure and organisation?	
How have you guided the reader/listener through the text? • Did you sample any reactions to your writing? • What was the response of your intended readership/listening audience?	
How did you use the feedback to change your text?	
Did you make any changes for any other reason? Give details.	
Have you noted your word counts?	

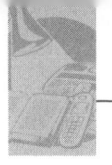

These guidelines should help you to start writing your own commentary, but you do not need to cover every aspect that they suggest. Worse still, you should not write something like: *'I have not used modern lexis; rhetorical features; narrative structure etc.'* It would be appropriate to refer to these omissions only if your style model has these features and there is a particular reason why you chose to leave them out of your own text.

You should remember two points:
- The commentary has a maximum word count of 1,500 words — you will not be able to write about everything. The best students focus on significant points, giving examples from their texts.
- The commentary is worth 50% of the marks in the coursework folder, so you need to spend time thinking about it and working on it. If you have written a first draft, then your teacher has something to work on when giving you advice on what to include and what to omit.

For further advice read the student commentaries (and the moderator comments) included in the next section of this guide.

Student Coursework

AS English Language & Literature

This section provides examples of texts submitted by students for their coursework folder. There are two reading texts with accompanying commentaries, one at A-grade and one at C-grade standard, and two listening texts with accompanying commentaries, again one at A-grade and one at C-grade standard.

Each of the student texts is accompanied by comments from a moderator, preceded by the icon *m*. These comments indicate the students' achievements and potential areas for development, explaining why an A or C grade would be awarded.

Each of the students whose work is used in this section discussed his/her AS coursework texts while in the A2 year and found that this evaluation helped when writing the text transformation coursework. The grade-C student for both the reading and listening audience resubmitted her folder using the same texts, and was able to improve her mark to a top grade B.

A-grade reading text

Magazine article

Author: Katie Lancaster
Purpose: Persuade
Audience: Readers of *Cosmopolitan* magazine

Video violence inciting tearaway teens?

It's all around us, on the news and in real life, as well as in films, video games and even the music we listen to. So why is it that violence in the media has been forced to take the rap for teenage delinquency and dysfunctional family life? Is it because the public strives to establish a link between apparently random acts of violence and the aggressive images we are undeniably bombarded with?

> The opening paragraph of this article works well — it follows a fairly ambiguous statement with two challenging questions. These are (as a journalistic piece should be) a summary of the article.

'Video nasty'

Horror and disgust swept the nation on 16 February 1993 when the body of little James Bulger was discovered. Video games were held responsible, stifling any doubt as to who was 'really' behind the murder of a little boy who never reached his third birthday. The 'Chucky doll' from *Child's Play* became almost as infamous as Ian Venables and Robert Thompson, the murderers themselves. Outrage was created among parents of impressionable children and the term 'video nasty' became synonymous with certain behaviours of disaffected youth.

> It seems a little strained to write about an event that took place in 1993, even though the case affected the whole nation. Since this text was submitted in 2005, a more recent example (such as any of the 'happy slapping' cases) could have been used to better effect. This would have made a more realistic reason for writing the article.

We all remember the graphic images of 20 April 1999 at Columbine High School, when student gunmen murdered 13 students and one teacher, and wounded a further 21 pupils. After the killing rampage the perpetrators, Eric Harris, 18, and Dylan Klebold, 17, turned the guns on themselves. President Clinton blamed video games, action movies and some popular songs of the time.

> This example illustrates the point being made.

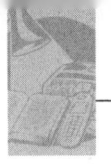

Fantasy vs reality

Religious groups expressed particular revulsion, and many branded the media with sole responsibility. In fact, these children had suffered tremendous mental anguish before they listened to Marilyn Manson or played Dungeons and Dragons. My suggestion is that we look closer at the real world before resorting to fantasy.

I'm not denying that these children have, rightly or wrongly, been exposed to violence in the media in their lifetime. I am however *convinced* that of all the contributing factors to violent behaviour, the mass media are far from the most dangerous. Perhaps a greater cause for concern (using the James Bulger case as an example), is the domestic violence commonplace in Venables' home, or the way these boys were bullied by their so-called friends. I for one know that when I listen to Marilyn Manson or watch *Boyz in the Hood* I am in no way inclined to emulate any acts of violence which have been depicted.

This comment has a personal voice an audience would relate to.

'Shocked and appalled'

Murder, natural disaster, suicide — the news is full of ghastly images that simply do not shock us any more. It is safe to say, however, that when the majority of us witness violence and abuse first hand, we are as shocked and appalled as we ever were. This is because during primary socialisation we are taught that there is a distinct difference between fantasy and reality. In this case, the media is the fantasy, and as a result it is possible to push boundaries.

As new shock tactics are unveiled in an attempt to capture the largest audience possible and make the most money, a moral panic is exposed. Society's ills, in this case inadequate parenting and an arguably ineffective disciplinary system in schools, are more likely to be contributing factors to the growing sociopathic tendencies in today's youth.

Schooling is commonly blamed in the media for deteriorating standards — Katie has obviously researched her style model well.

Nevertheless, as headlines reveal more and more horrific stories, the now accustomed stigma of scenes of violence in the media is attached. An example of this is the murder of Michael Moss, aged 15, who was doused in petrol and had his ear sliced off by a school gang in Liverpool. His murder was said to resemble the final scene in the controversial classic *Reservoir Dogs*. A well-known 'certificate 18', the film caused outrage and a familiar scapegoat was resurrected. The general concern for the public was the availability of such films and the detrimental impact they had on children and teens alike. My concern is what had really driven these boys, school children, to kill.

An interesting 'concern' is posed here.

AQA (B) Unit 3

'Brainwashing'

The influence of the cultivating media surrounds us and we are aware of its beneficial and damaging effects. The creation of murderers, however, is not one of them. We have the ability to acquire information and decide for ourselves whether or not an action is moral. Our opinions will differ in accordance with our social background, but unless you are from a far-off tribe that hunts and kills strangers, then you, like me, would not think of instigating an attack on another human being.

We can all feel anger or frustration and desire a cathartic outlet. Some people express this verbally, or go for a run. Computer games, despite their supposed satanic influences, allow similar escapism. There is a certain degree of pleasure to be taken in blowing your opponent to smithereens, however, this is not to be taken literally!

No child is born with the instinct to kill. | Picture of little devil |

And to use the words of Quentin Tarantino: 'Violence as an aesthetic form can be beautiful.'

📝 Tarantino's words are used effectively to support the argument.

If it's not inciting you and me, why them?

📝 The article ends by challenging the reader to agree with the writer.

Word count: 824

📝 **The magazine article is well written. Katie has a confident voice and her argument is sustained (AO4). She is not sidetracked but keeps her focus on the view that films do not incite copycat violence. There is a clear sense of the target audience being addressed (and provoked to reflective thought). Katie has an assured control over the genre (AO6) and has selected the magazine *Cosmopolitan* as a style model because she wanted to provoke a thoughtful response. There is sophisticated control of the written language (AO6).**

This text was awarded a mark in the centre of the top band (26–30 marks).

■ ■ ■

Commentary on magazine article

There have been many changes in the approach taken in teenage girls' and women's magazines over recent years. However, the influence is still largely based on superficial beauty and celebrities. This is why I wanted to create the kind of article I believe a magazine aimed at woman aged 21–30 *should* contain, being careful to maintain the style of my chosen genre. I have written a magazine article for the women's magazine *Cosmopolitan* about the possible links between violence in the media and violence in teenagers, in order to persuade the audience to consider possible alternatives for motives behind such behaviour. I felt an opinionated article would be an ideal medium for capturing the attention of the reader.

> The beginning of this paragraph is an over-generalisation. It would have been useful for Katie to have undertaken specific market research, which would have resulted in a more informed overview. Katie should also have informed the reader of why she chose that particular 'opinionated' topic (e.g. was it because of an incident in the media or previous study of sociology or media?)

Although taking a different approach to conventional women's magazines, it was important that I used *Cosmopolitan* as a style model and studied the articles it contained to ensure I emulated the style of the genre sufficiently well. I wanted to capture the attention of my audience at a glance so an eye-catching question with the use of alliteration here provided a more memorable caption. I also used declarative and interrogative sentences which challenged the reader.

> More detail of the style model is needed in this paragraph. The language point about declaratives and interrogatives is excellent, but needs to be supported by specific examples.

By conveying my own views in the article it would be easier for the reader to generate an opinion, which hopefully mirrors mine. By using emotive language such as 'horror and disgust swept the nation' I also hoped to stir any maternal instinct, which would then persuade the readers or strengthen their opinion.

> The lexis does not specifically evoke 'maternal instinct'. It is important to remember that *Cosmopolitan* is not aimed at a 'maternal' readership but at career-minded women who have perhaps put motherhood on hold.

I tried to convey a sense of voice in my writing as I discovered that magazines strive constantly to establish a relationship with their audience through language use. I used lists of three 'Murder, natural disaster, suicide' to persuade the audience of the strength of my argument. I was careful to keep the tone of my article conversational, using words such as 'teen', as I found that abbreviations like these are common to these magazines. As I had referred to the beliefs of certain religious groups, 'branding the media with sole responsibility' for the abandonment of morals, I later used language to link to this as 'satanic'. By using pronouns such as in 'we are taught', the reader is encouraged to feel involved in the content of the article. For my final sentence I wanted to use a rhetorical question, as a last attempt to persuade the reader of my argument.

> This point made in the opening sentence of this paragraph is established well in the article. Although the 'list of three' technique does not persuade by itself, it is a device used in persuasive writing. The point about the use of abbreviations is a good one. Are there any other examples that Katie could have given? She should have discussed the ending of the article. A stronger and more permissive stance could have been argued for, if her line of reasoning was followed.

I knew that I was writing a relatively lengthy article, so it was important that I divided it into manageable sections. I assessed the structure of several magazine articles, and then my own, in order to make the necessary changes. I wanted to make the article link horrific images that were portrayed in the media by the James Bulger case with more recent graphic images. The Columbine High School made a good link because President Clinton had named violent movies and video games specifically as contributing factors. Having set up these and the opinion of 'religious groups', I could introduce my own personal voice. Tarantino's *Reservoir Dogs* is an underlying theme for the final section of the article, since it is always associated with demands for censorship and it allowed me to pose my final, thought-provoking question. I decided to add captions to mirror the style of a magazine which entices and maintains the attention of its readership. In order to emulate *Cosmopolitan* it was necessary for me to have between one and five pictures. I chose to use one picture which illustrated the point I was making in my penultimate paragraph: 'No child is born with the instinct to kill.' I lifted the picture from www.google.com/images, where I typed in 'little devil'.

> As Katie implies, the length of this piece — at about 800 words — is probably the maximum for such an article. The discussion of the structure of the article shows that Katie is able to explain how the content of the article was planned — this helps her achieve high marks. The discussion of graphology and page layout at the end of the paragraph is a less important aspect of language use, although it explains how Katie replicated the style model.

Although using a formal register, I was careful not to use vocabulary which alienated the expected audience for *Cosmopolitan*. This maintains as wide an audience as possible without the patronising tone of other women's magazines. I decided to talk briefly about a few examples of violent crimes, rather than discuss one or two stories in detail as I am assuming the reader is already aware of the cases I used to illustrate my argument.

> Examples should have been given of vocabulary used to prevent alienation of the readers. The last sentence of this paragraph is a valid point and supports Katie's thoughtful planning.

I believe my final piece succeeded in presenting a strong argument and, on the whole, was effectively persuasive.

Word count: 700

> **The strength of this commentary is the understanding that Katie shows of how she has structured her text to persuade the audience to consider her own opinion. She shows a good understanding of vocabulary choices and the tone that is being captured (AO4). She has a very good awareness of choices relevant to the genre of a magazine article and its intended purpose (AO5). Her comments about the purpose and audience of the text show that she knew what she was aiming to achieve (AO6).**

Although Katie has written to a good standard, there are gaps in the commentary which need to be filled by giving specific examples and explaining her understanding of the style model.

This commentary was awarded a mark in the middle of the 21–25 band. For her text and commentary, Katie achieved an overall grade **A**.

C-grade reading text

Brochure

Author: Maya McCourt
Purpose: Persuade
Audience: 18-year-olds

Make your mark! Vote!

You've just turned 18. You realise you have this thing called the 'vote', which supposedly lets you have a say as to how this country's run. What's it going to do? Why should you vote? And if you do vote, who should you vote for?

Why should you vote?

Today's Britain is run by one main political party. This party is voted in by having the majority of votes in lots of different areas called 'constituencies'. Each constituency normally has at least three people standing. The person with the most votes will become a member of parliament. The political party with the most people in parliament will be in power.

Does the text need to explain 'constituencies' to its target audience?

Simple as that.

All you have to do is vote for the person or party that you most agree with.

Each political party has a manifesto which you can check out on the internet and, very often, watching the news tells you what the parties are running for.

It would have been helpful to have included website addresses of the main political parties.

So, all the politicians tell you that voting is really important. True, they're all egomaniacs that think you'd have voted for them if you'd actually voted, but it's more than just that. Voting is important for all sorts of different reasons:

- Britain is a democratic society. To be a truly democratic society, it has to have people voting. Sure, your vote is one of millions, but sometimes the difference between a win and a loss can be just a dozen or so votes. Also, remember — you're voting for someone in your constituency. The number of votes involved in that is far fewer, and each and every vote is important.

> *📝 A reference to other countries in which there is no opportunity to have a say in how the country is run could reinforce this concept of democracy. It may also be relevant to indicate, by contrast, that to have the vote is a privilege.*

- There is a history of unjust systems before this one. Think of the suffragettes, who went through terrible hardships — prison, force-feeding and much more — so that women could have an equal say. It's not just them either. Back in the 1800s only a tiny minority could vote, and it wasn't until 1967 that everybody over the age of 18 could. It would be a shame to throw away the vote that they fought so hard for.

> *📝 This reference to 'unjust systems' needs clarification. Are these in the UK? Maya should have developed the historical aspect by indicating who the 'tiny minority' of the 1800s were and who were the last to gain the vote in 1967.*

- There are big differences between the policies of even the main parties, not to mention the smaller ones. The party that gets into power has a big effect on this country, and it up to you to decide whether that effect would be good or not. If the Conservatives get in, they're going to be massively different from the Liberal Democrats, or even Labour.

And last but not least...

- The media are not always right! So, the *Sun* might say that Party X is definitely going to win, but does that mean they will? Not for certain.

What would happen if you didn't vote?

Imagine that Party X is standing in your area. The media say that there is no way this party could get in, because everybody hates them, right? So, you think, 'Sorted, I don't need to vote'. So you don't. Polling day comes and goes. The results come out, and shock! The MP for your area is a member of Party X. This person is supposedly taking your views to parliament and you don't agree with them at all. What's more, they only got in by a few dozen votes. That would mean that if only you and your mates had voted, there'd be a different MP in parliament.

Okay, so that might not be true for your area, but voting is still just as important.

Think of another situation...

You're a student — if you voted, you'd vote for Party X. But you think this party's education policy is awful. You're not the only one, either. Now, if Party X finds out that it's losing all these votes to another political party because of education, it might revise its policy. If it thinks you aren't going to vote anyway, what would be the point in changing it?

> *📝 A leaflet written to encourage students to vote in general should not attempt to influence the audience to vote in a specific way. A reader of this brochure might be able to guess which party Maya is referring to, moving the focus of the brochure away from 'Use your vote' towards 'Vote for this party' or even 'Don't vote for that*

AQA (B) Unit 3

party'. This misunderstanding of the real purpose of such a brochure would reduce the mark that this piece would achieve.

You must always remember — your vote *will* make a difference.

Word count: 675

M Maya has written a text that is generally well matched to its audience (18-year-olds) and form (a brochure). The purpose is not one of neutral persuasion (see above) — this shows an insecure understanding of purpose, and would therefore fulfil **AO4** at **C** grade. Maya has chosen a straightforward genre, which she has written competently, but her text lacks subtlety — this fulfils **AO6** at grade **C**.

This text was awarded a mark at the top of the 11–15 band, although it had the potential to be improved (which is what Maya did in her resubmission).

■ ■ ■

Commentary on brochure

For my reading audience English coursework, I decided to create the text for a brochure talking about voting. Its purpose is primarily to persuade 18-year-olds to vote, as well as giving them a small amount of information on the voting system.

Its target audience is 18-year-olds who are not thinking of voting in the forthcoming general election. Although I have discussed the suffragettes, it is not gender specific, as the problem of voter apathy lies with both sexes. It does not require the reader to have any

M This paragraph is incomplete. Careful proofreading would have picked this up before the text was submitted.

I decided to write about voter apathy, as it has become a big problem in this country, and the forthcoming general election makes it relevant. It was written to appeal to those who have little knowledge of the voting system, and those with little desire to vote, simply through apathy.

I based this piece on the numerous brochures and leaflets that I have seen in my college, all trying to induce the reader to think about universities, or career choices etc. Because I started my coursework as an article, my influences changed. I realised that an article was not quite the style I wanted, and I also wanted to do something more positive than just blame voter apathy on certain things. The original draft of my text, the article, seemed to disagree with the final draft of my brochure, in that I concluded that 'when people start to vote, that's when I'll be getting worried'. However, I do think that people should vote, even if they are happy with the way things are. I changed my piece from an article to a brochure because I thought the style of writing that I did fitted better with a brochure.

📝 This section makes valid points, but it needs a more succinct style.

My style of writing is informal and conversational.

📝 Maya should have explained how she established this discourse between the writer and reader. Citing expressions such as 'just turned' and 'this thing' from her opening paragraph would explain this.

This means that it could be aimed at a teenage audience without worry of alienating any of them by using overly complicated lexis of a strict, formal style of writing. This is particularly important, because I wanted to persuade people to vote, and so alienating them would have been disastrous. The language style aims to create a rapport with the reader by using conversational phrases, such as 'everybody hates them, right?' and relating back to the reader by using the impersonal pronoun — 'Why should *you* vote' and '*You*'ve just turned 18'.

📝 Maya's point about using a conversational tone to create a rapport is a good one. However, she has made a linguistic error in this paragraph. The impersonal pronoun is not used. 'You' is the second-person pronoun.

The tone is informal with varied sentence lengths.

📝 Although varied sentence lengths would have been ideal, Maya has in fact used little variety in the text except the short sentences 'And last but not least' and 'Think of another situation'.

Bullet points and subheadings break up the text, making it more readable and drawing the eye more to it.

It is simple and to the point — if it was a long block of text it would make it much harder to read, and therefore put many people off. It is meant to be easy and quick to read, but giving the reader something to think about, persuading them to vote.

📝 This section does not add anything to the analysis since it deals with the look of the text (the graphology).

When redrafting, I decided to cut up the piece a bit more, to make it easier to read. I also decided to change the syntax, as I had made the style too conversational. For example, 'Imagine if, in your area, a party you really don't agree with is standing. Say, for example, Party X' — I changed this to 'Imagine Party X is standing in your area', which is far shorter, more to the point, and easier to read. I added the subheadings to break up the text and to make it easier to understand and included a positive end line, so that the reader could go away with that in mind: 'your vote *will* make a difference'. I also gave it the title 'Make your mark' as a pun that would be remembered easily and would also catch the eye of someone who is perhaps browsing through a few brochures.

📝 This last comment about the pun in the title offers a good explanation of why the title was chosen.

I think that I succeeded in what I set out to accomplish. In a second attempt I would have produced it in a brochure style, along with pictures and different fonts. I would also have looked more into brochures that have been published for young people so that the style became more apparent.

You are not judged on the graphology of your text but on the appropriateness of the language you have used. In her resubmission, Maya made minor alterations to the graphology of her text but concentrated on the content and received a good mark. In any written task like this, you should gain greater understanding of your style model by looking at as many examples as possible.

However, I think that it is brief and to the point, as well as offering a sound argument as to why you should vote.

Word count: 600

Maya has made some valid points, but her commentary should have discussed the techniques used to persuade her intended audience — the language chosen and the 'signposts' within the text to direct the reader. These signposts were present in Maya's text — they included expressions such as 'simple as that'; 'so'; 'last but not least'; 'what would happen if you didn't vote?'. These are effective persuasive tools, as they lead the reader to the same opinion as the writer.

This commentary was awarded a mark at the bottom of the 16–20 band.

A-grade listening text

Television transcript

Author: Culain Wood
Purpose: Persuade
Audience: Viewers of television holiday programmes

Kinvara and surrounding area

PROGRAMME PRESENTER: Now we're going to Culain Wood, looking at an unexpected break on the West Coast of Ireland.

SECONDARY PRESENTER (CULAIN WOOD):

A number of different locations are used, and this is appropriate for a television transcript. It gives the viewer visual stimulation. Kinvara is a real place, described below by Culain as 'the most beautiful place I know', which is why he chose to persuade television holiday viewers to consider making a visit.

[Standing in front of ferry]
A holiday in Ireland is never a one-off thing, like, for instance, a fortnight in the Costa Blanca, for if you visit Ireland once, you go back. And as it's only a ferry ride or a very cheap plane journey away, you can now go as often as you'd like to, which for me, would be every day! [Steps on to ferry]

[Sitting in ferry drinks lounge]
For me, the West Coast seems to have a sort of lure that very few people can turn down, and Ireland has far much more to offer in my opinion than any all-inclusive resort and if you're like me, and you like to set off to explore on your own, in your own time, there is nowhere better than the West Coast, in particular, Kinvara. [Turns to waiter and takes drink] Ah, thank you.

[Standing in front of dry stone wall]
As soon as you arrive on the West Coast, there are a few distinguishing features that you'll notice that define Ireland...like perhaps the well-organised transport system.
[Points to collection of road signs all jumbled together]
For me though, only one sign on here is important. No, not this one.
[Points to sign for pub]
But this one.
[Points to sign for Kinvara]
As the fishing town of Kinvara is quite probably my favourite place on the whole West Coast.

📝 This section works well. It has the feel of stage-managed, pre-recorded clips that feature in all holiday programmes.

I'm in Kinvara, on Galway Bay, where one of the attractions has to be the beautiful landscape and views. If you won't take my word for it, take a look for yourself.

[*Points to ocean view and camera looks out to sea*]

📝 There is an understanding of how text is used to include the listening (and obviously viewing) audience. The visuals are presented for the listeners to judge for themselves.

The first thing you're likely to notice about Kinvara is the sheer number of pubs it has to offer! Eleven! And that's just those around the quay! If you like a drink, look no further than Keogh's, Sexton's, Tully's, Green's, need I go on?

[*Sitting outside pub with pint of Guinness*]
Whatever time of year you choose to come here, you're never short of activities. Two huge festivals take place in Kinvara each year, the 'Fleadh na gCuach' or the festival of music, and the 'Cruinniu na mBad' or the festival of the boats. These take place around Easter and early autumn, so I'd advise you to book early if you're planning to come during one of those periods. Summer is hectic as well with the Galway races and with everywhere within 50 miles of the racecourse fully booked, you'll need to get in early in Kinvara. Although the relatively large numbers of people at these times may put you off somewhat, anyone with experience of the festivals or the races will tell you you'd be mad to miss out.
[*Raises pint glass and reel of shots of festivals and races comes on for a few minutes*]

📝 Culain could have told viewers the exact dates of the two festivals.

[*Walking along quay*]
Once you're in Kinvara, you may want to stay put, but if you find time, it's well worth a drive to see what's on offer outside of the village. The Burren is incredibly impressive and you're free to roam if you'd like.
[*Shot of presenter standing on burren*]

📝 It might be useful to indicate exactly what 'The Burren' is.

Or for natural history enthusiasts like myself, you could choose to experience the caves and take a look at the bear bones.
[*Shot of presenter with torchlight on helmet looking into bear den*]

A little further along the coast road, after stopping at the occasional set of sand dunes for jumping off, you'll find the cliffs of Moher and, well, I'll let you make your own mind up.
[*Shot of presenter standing on cliff edge as camera zooms out revealing impressive view of cliffs*]

📝 Again, this is a good technique to include the audience.

69

[*Shot of presenter walking up pavement*]
Back in Kinvara, if you're short of a car, there's always a tour or even a banquet fit for a king, or tourist in the very impressive Dungaire castle.
[*Shot of presenter walking up to castle*]
Trust me, it won't disappoint.
[*Presenter takes a drink from cup and turns to the stage in the banquet room*]

[*Sitting in a living room in front of roaring fire drinking tea*]
Now, if you're wondering where to stay, you can't really go wrong, though I would recommend a smaller B&B such as this one where the owners become friends and really do make you feel at home.
[*Presenter gestures to owner to pour his tea and owner replies*]
OWNER OF B&B: Ah, get it yourself.
[*Presenter turns to camera and smirks*]

So, after a busy day on the Burren or out for a walk, you leave the kids in the comfortable hands of your hosts and set off in search of a meal. It won't take you long before you're tucking in to a beautiful menu. The Pier Head in Kinvara, although a little expensive, makes a perfect one-off meal on your holiday, catering for whatever tickles your fancy.

> This is a little tactless. The television station would not want to have to deal with outraged owners.

[*Cuts into and takes a bite of steak in the restaurant*]
If it's everyday feeding you're looking for, try somewhere like the Lobster Bar a mile or two out of the village where fantastic food is relatively cheap, and the Guinness isn't bad either
[*Takes a drink from pint glass*]

[*Walking through village*]
So, whatever you decide to do here, you can't go far wrong. What is definite is that you'll want to come back again and again. And what is fantastic is that no matter how many times you come back, it will never be the same. That is with the exception, of course, of the Guinness, which is always a pleasure to be savoured. Go on then, just one more. [*Nods to the camera and walks into pub*]

> The use of short utterances here is an excellent technique when scripting for a listening audience. Look at how the sentences are non-standard, but the end result is that it sounds natural. This is excellent scripting.

PROGRAMME PRESENTER: That was Culain Wood, in Kinvara on the West Coast of Ireland.

Word count: 947

> This text for a listening audience has an authentic tone that is perfectly matched to a *Holiday*-type programme (AO4). Culain has crafted the text for a television

AQA (B) Unit 3

audience; he is aware of the demands of the visual medium and the way that text is used to persuade the audience that Kinvara should be visited. He has sustained a high level of written English and has balanced the use of a style model with the originality (and personal knowledge) of the location (AO6).

Culain's listening text was marked in the middle of the top band (26–30 marks).

■ ■ ■

Commentary on television transcript

This television transcript, which is intended for a holiday programme, includes the features that such programmes can be expected to contain. The piece conveys the presenter's individual opinions and attitudes while also providing the audience with information on the reviewed area. These two conventions are generic for programmes such as *Holiday* and (to some extent) *Wish you were here* which is why I included examples such as 'one of the attractions has to be the beautiful landscape and views. If you won't take my word for it, take a look for yourself', which clearly voices the presenter's opinion while allowing the viewers to make their own minds up.

> There is scope for Culain to indicate his personal knowledge of the area, which (when asked) he described as his favourite place in the whole world.

Television programmes such as *Holiday* have an audience that is mainly family based and they focus on this through the presenter's identity and attitudes. Statements such as 'you leave the kids in the comfortable hands of your hosts...' and 'sheer number of pubs it has to offer!' clearly show that the presenter is a working adult, as he refers to having children and enjoying a holiday drink.

The main purpose of a programme like this is to advertise a particular holiday destination and highlight the good points of places with phrases such as 'The Burren is incredibly impressive', but features of the transcript such as the banter between presenter and B&B owner and the visual jokes about the road signs give an entertaining aspect to the text.

> Culain could have written about the persuasive language he has used in the script. This is evident in the way he contrasted Kinvara with the typical holiday in Costa Blanca, his use of positive references to all aspects of Kinvara and its surrounding area, and the invitation he gives to viewers to make up their own mind when shown visual attractions.

In order to make sure that my style and tone were accurate and appropriate I watched an episode of *Holiday* and in particular a review of a family holiday destination in which each member of the family was addressed in turn. I think I have incorporated this within my piece with the mention of activities such as 'a tour or even a banquet fit for a king, or tourist in the very impressive Dungaire castle' and 'sand dunes for

AS English Language & Literature

jumping off'. I feel that different members of the family are each informed of what is potentially on offer to them at the destination.

Before I arrived at a transcript that I felt satisfied the requirements of a holiday review I redrafted twice, initially altering certain uses of language and tone and finally altering the structure. The process of moving from first draft to second draft involved certain linguistic changes such as the change from 'I'm in Kinvara, on Galway bay and for those of you who enjoy beautiful ocean views, let this speak for itself' to 'I'm in Kinvara, on Galway bay, where one of the attractions has to be the beautiful landscape and views. If you won't take my word for it, take a look for yourself', which I felt was necessary as it has changed from a rather bland comment to one which highlights the subject as 'one of the attractions'.

I feel that an important part of a transcript such as this is to achieve an appropriate tone, one which provides information, but does so in an entertaining way. One entertaining linguistic device typical to this genre is sarcasm, which is used in 'like perhaps the well-organised transport system', which highlights certain romantic elements of the place being reviewed.

> The word 'sarcasm' is perhaps too strong. It is a humorous comment.

If this were a radio transcript, the dialogue would have to be over-descriptive but as this is for television, a great deal can be left to the images on the screen. I have indicated these instructions by using brackets and italics to clearly distinguish them from the spoken dialogue.

> Culain is showing a good understanding of the demands for scripting for television and offers an explanation of how the visual images work.

With the availability of images I was able to include dialogue that would be explained by the on-screen images, this is why the phrase 'points to' is used a lot as a reference to the dialogue. Another element of the redrafting process was to improve the structure and in the final draft structure. The fact that each stage direction is on a separate line creates clarity and order within the piece.

> Culain could have explained how he structured the text in terms of selection of locations.

Overall, I feel that because I have used a specific style model aimed at a particular target audience, I have created a transcript suitable for a programme such as *Holiday*.

Word count: 680

> Culain's commentary shows a good awareness of writing for a persuasive purpose and the targeted audience, with a clear explanation of tone and style **(AO4)**. He could have given more indication of what he had achieved in terms of making the text appropriate for a listening audience through syntax and grammatical choices **(AO5)**, but he did make effective use of a style model. He has a good understanding of the effects made in the drafting process **(AO6)** and

analysed his text in a thoughtful way, showing that he understood the process of writing.

There was scope for Culain to improve the commentary by giving specific examples. However, he was awarded a mark in the 26–30 band (at the lower end) because he showed a good understanding of how the language in script works and of the genre and audience for the script.

C-grade listening text

Radio script

Author: Maya McCourt
Purpose: Entertain
Audience: Radio drama

Inside the House: a radio play

[*Inside a house.*]

📝 How can this be conveyed to a radio audience?

[*Sound of keys in door. Door opens and closes.*]
[*Sue enters.*]

📝 How can this be conveyed to a radio audience? The character must be addressed by name.

DENNIS: Hello dear.

📝 Maya could have scripted 'Sue, was that you?' to help the audience identify Sue.

[*Sound of general tidying, movement of objects as Sue searches for a book.*]

SUE: Hmmm?

DENNIS: [*pointedly*] I said, hello dear.

SUE: [*still moving around, searching*] Oh, yes, hello darling.

DENNIS: Having a good day?

SUE: [*distracted*] I'm fine, [*voice fading, as if from another room*] but where is that bloody book?

📝 This was an opportunity to identify Dennis by name.

[*Pause while we can hear the rattle of objects being displaced and Sue's footsteps.*]

DENNIS: You know, once upon a time people took notice of me. Life was good. [*as if in a reverie*] When I was younger I used to live in a grand house. [*pause*] I loved that house.

SUE: [*mind not really on what she's saying*] What's that you say? If I'm hearing correctly it seems you're even lying to yourself these days.

AQA (B) Unit 3

DENNIS: [*ignoring her*] I had a cat as well you know. One of the ugly ones with the squashed faces. [*pauses, as if thinking*] Desperately expensive, and we only kept it to kick.

📝 This is a good use of ironic comment — it allows the audience to realise that they cannot assume that everything Dennis says is true.

SUE: [*sarcastic*] Ah yes, of course. And you had a helicopter pad on the roof as well, no doubt. I'm just off out, by the way.

DENNIS: [*sarcastic*] What? So soon? And don't be silly, helicopter pads had no class. [*yawns*] You dragged me down.

SUE: I'm sure I did no such thing. How did I figure in this delusional fantasy?

DENNIS: [*offhand*] You didn't…I had a mistress.

📝 If Maya is trying to convey that Dennis and Sue's marriage is not as it should be, there needs to be some sort of retort from Sue.

SUE: [*mildly put out*] Yes, well.

Ah hah! I've found it. Right, I'm off. Things to do. I'd say you knew how it was…but you don't. If anybody could make you do anything you didn't want to, I'd say it was a miracle.

📝 What is happening here? Has Dennis retired and Sue is still working? Has he always had money and never needed to work? There is clearly conflict here, but the audience does not know what it is.

DENNIS: But of course sweets, however would I live, otherwise? I'm sure it would be most repressive. Stay and do the same.

SUE: Oh honestly. You're not going to forget Marie's funeral, are you?

📝 There needs to be a time context here, such as 'I'll see you at the crematorium at 1:30'.

DENNIS: [*mock horror*] Would I ever?

SUE: Don't say that. Where were you at Joseph's wedding then? He was most looking forward to seeing you.

📝 This last expression is clumsy. Perhaps it should be more laboured, e.g. 'you managed to forget that'.

DENNIS: Nonsense. Anyway, weddings are such dull occasions…

SUE: Yes, well, you're coming to this funeral, even if only for Robert's sake.

DENNIS: Why? He's not going to be there.

SUE: [*sounding annoyed*] You know why that is. Really, Dennis, you are coming and that is that.

📝 It might help the audience if they knew why Dennis has to go.

DENNIS: Oh very well. Though I would have thought they could've let him out just for a day. It is his wife's funeral, after all.

SUE: You know very well that her death is the reason for him being in prison. We all know he didn't do it. It just might take a bit more time in court, that's all. Meanwhile, you are coming. I want to see you in a suit as well. Poor Yvonne last year was very shocked.

📝 Sue's comments sound unnatural. A script for a listening audience should sound like natural speech. The reference to Yvonne means nothing to the audience. It would have been better to say, 'and don't turn up looking scruffy like you normally do!', before the instruction to wear a suit, rather than refer to yet another character who is not introduced in the play script.

DENNIS: [sighs] Oh fine.

SUE: Anyway, I have to be going. I've got people to see...

📝 This is a cliché. No one says this except in a light-hearted way, making a joke of how busy they are.

DENNIS: [interrupts] Ah, but I don't.

SUE: Well, don't say that was ever my fault.

[Sound of door closing as Sue exits. Creak of chair.]

DENNIS: [settles back, stretches] And it was such a lovely house.

📝 The audience may not understand that Dennis is referring back to the fantasy of his earlier life. It would have been more of a comment on his marriage if he said 'and it was such a happy marriage', with an emphasis on the past tense.

[Complete silence, indicating a change of scene. Sound of funeral fades up — rattle of cups and saucers, quiet murmur of guests.]

MOURNER: [quiet voice] It must be a hard time for you.

DENNIS: [mouth full, chewing] Yes, yes. Shocking how bad caterers are these days. You'd think they could at least put something decent on for a funeral. Oh well, we may as well make the best of it.

MOURNER: [sounding uncomfortable] Well, yes, yes. But your poor wife. She wasn't young...well, I'm so sorry.

📝 This reference to the age of the wife does not make sense.

DENNIS: On the contrary, I think I've done rather well, considering.

MOURNER: But...

DENNIS: [*continuing*] I mean, a chance like that doesn't come along too often. Seize it by the throat as you might say. [*gives a short laugh*]

MOURNER: [*gives a nervous laugh*] Well...umm...yes.

DENNIS: I had a teacher back in primary school — or was it secondary? I'm never quite sure about these things — who always said that. Mind you, it was a Catholic school, and he was a priest so we never used to know what he meant. Of course, him saying it in Latin never helped. Used to say it before he hit us. Carpe jugulum. Great man, great man.

📝 There is humour in the fact that the funeral guest confuses Dennis with the husband of the deceased, but Dennis's comments make no sense, especially the reference to 'a chance' and his memories of school. If Dennis had continued as if he were referring to Sue and his 'lost' relationship, this humour might have been more successful. At this point, the audience would have lost track of the plot and may switch off to the rest of the play.

MOURNER: I...yes...indeed, my deepest condolences. [*moves away*]

SUE: Funny, that man seemed to think you were Robert...

DENNIS: Oh did he really? And I was so sure he was talking about us getting married. I'm just so proud of you, you understand. Anyway, he must be very ill-informed, considering.

📝 Is Dennis proud of Sue? Nothing has indicated this up until this point.

SUE: You knew perfectly well what he thought. You're just so uncaring. I don't know why I married you at all, sometimes.

DENNIS: Oh, don't you dear? I always thought it was because you were pregnant.

📝 This sort of comment is indicative of resentment and of a marriage that is at the point of breaking up.

SUE: Now stop that. That was simply incidental, and I am not having an argument at poor Marie's funeral.

📝 Clearly there have been other arguments.

DENNIS: No, no. You wouldn't want me doing to you what Robert did to her. Mind you, I don't think I could ever be bothered with prison.

SUE: Ssshhh! This is not the place. It was merely an unfortunate accident.

DENNIS: Yes, I always thought it was rather bad luck that she decided to fall down those stairs just at the moment that would incriminate him. I'm sure it was just coincidence. Still, pity he couldn't be here.

📝 This tells the audience what happened, but it does not seem logical that Dennis would add 'Still, pity he couldn't be here'. Does Dennis despise Robert, or does he envy him?

Sue: Hmmm...

📝 Sue's response is not believable. If she thought that Robert was innocent, she would react more strongly.

Dennis: [*continuing*] Make sure she was really dead. Ah, what a wonderful institution marriage is, I'm sure.

Word count: 955

📝 Maya has attempted an imaginative listening text, and she shows some awareness of the genre conventions of writing for radio (AO6). However, the dialogue is stilted and does not ring true. The plot lacks a clear focus and the end result is rather dull, has no clear sense of development and gives the audience little insight into the relationships of the characters involved (AO4).

Maya was rewarded for her understanding of the demands of scripting for a listening audience and for making an imaginative attempt at writing a radio play. The text was awarded a mark at the top of the 16–20 band (a high grade C).

■ ■ ■

Commentary on radio script

For my listening audience coursework, I decided to do a short radio drama, to be played on Radio 4 as one of a series.

📝 The aim of a 'series' is too ambitious for a coursework text.

Its target audience is from 40 to 60 as the characters are quite old, and the humour is quite toned down — not intended, perhaps, to make one laugh out loud.

📝 It is often best to identify when a play would be aired rather than consider the actual range of the target audience. There are many people in the 40–60 age range who would not be interested in listening to a radio play, even though it concerned characters from their own age range.

My inspiration for *Inside the House* came from the Tom Stoppard play, *The Real Thing*. I liked the way his male characters were quite detached, and able to make witty observations that would otherwise be very emotive. For example, 'I always thought it was because you were pregnant' could be a very emotive phrase — Dennis is telling his wife he thinks that she married him because she was pregnant and not because she loved him. This is, though, not true. He is simply trying to wind her up in an offhand manner, and she knows it. Despite my play being for radio, I think it is aimed at the same audience.

📝 The first sentence of this paragraph displays a good knowledge of the style model. It would have been useful to indicate an example of a similar insensitive comment made by one of Stoppard's characters. However, Maya does not show clearly Sue's refusal to be wound up, as she claims, and the meaning of the last sentence of this paragraph is unclear.

The script aims to achieve downplayed humour, in that Dennis acts like he doesn't know what's going on, and that he lives in a world of his own, but in fact he is quite observant and hides his emotions. Following plays in the series could be about how he comes to terms with his displays of lack of emotion, and perhaps regrets it.

> The first sentence of this paragraph is an ambitious goal to achieve in an AS text and Maya would be credited for having thought about characterisation.

The language that Dennis uses is of a formal register, because he is quite upper class. He uses upper-class phrases, or upper-middle-class phrases such as ' Shocking, how bad' and 'I'm sure it would be most repressive'. The use of the word 'most' instead of 'very' is a formal way of speaking. I think there is opportunity for the relationship to be expanded and deepened in further plays in the series. There is an obvious affection between the two characters, seen through their affable arguments and the way Dennis is annoyed when Sue doesn't acknowledge him.

> Maya's comments about Dennis's use of the formal register are successful because she is looking at how she has crafted language to portray the social class of her character. She could also have given an example of Dennis's subtle sarcasm here. Candidates often make suggestions regarding what they *could* have done when they feel their text has not achieved the effect that they attempted. This probably indicates that Maya does not feel she has been particularly successful. She should have redrafted her text to expand the relationship between Dennis and Sue. The last sentence in this paragraph makes a good point, although it is a little unconvincing.

The play is set in two scenes — the first, developed scene where we are introduced to the characters and their relationship is established, and a second which puts them in a situation and explores their reactions. In further plays they could be put into more situations, as well as perhaps introducing other characters of more depth than, for example, the 'mourner'.

> Maya gives a good explanation here of how the play is structured, although the success of this structure is less certain. It is not profitable to speculate in the commentary about what you could write in the future. In the 750 words available, Maya should have focused on the language she used and what she achieved in her text.

In my redrafts, I linked the two scenes together, as when I got reader feedback it became apparent that it was not clear what was going on, either in the first or the second scene. I added more stage directions to remedy this.

> It is good practice to obtain feedback and to redraft as a result. It would have been useful to give the text to an 'expert' (e.g. a drama student) to examine it as a possible drama production. Such feedback would be informed and probably give more specific feedback than 'It's not clear what's going on'.

To an extent, *Inside the House* plays to character stereotypes as an element of comedy — Dennis as the henpecked husband and Sue the busy wife. However, they are not completely stereotypical, which gives the opportunity, perhaps, to explore their flaws and perhaps even make them more human.

> Contrary to what Maya has written, Dennis is not portrayed as the stereotype of the henpecked husband. The purpose of any drama is to place characters in a situation and explore their nature to give an insight that will reveal something to the audience. If you do not do this, the drama will probably be mundane and Maya has failed to fulfil this purpose.

I think, overall, that this radio play has been quite effective — I have received good feedback. However, if I was to do it again, I would perhaps give the characters a bit more depth — something to work on for future plays in the series. I would also look at a wider selection of authors, and maybe also at some radio plays, because *The Real Thing* is a play written for the stage.

Word count: 573

> It is always useful to indicate constructive criticism from a knowledgeable and informed audience. In this section, Maya has indicated that, in effect, she was halfway through the process of writing a successful play. If she had followed her own suggestions, her end product would have been more effective.

> There is a range of comments here, but they are more descriptive than analytical (AO4), for example when Maya writes about the feedback she obtained and what her aims were in scripting the play. She makes some comments about the language used, and indicates how the text should work (AO5), when she describes the relationship between Dennis and Sue, although this does not work as she had intended. She also comments on the changes made in the drafting process (AO6) when she writes: 'I linked the two scenes together', but does not develop this point. The commentary is short — it is permissible to write up to 750 words for each commentary and Maya could have used this space to expand on certain points.

> This commentary is weaker than the text it accompanies and was given a mark towards the bottom of the 11–15 band, showing some competence at grade D. Maya's text and commentary together just achieved a grade C.